India at 70

India at 70: Multidisciplinary Approaches examines Indian independence in August 1947 and its multiple afterlives. With nine contributions by a range of international scholars, it interrogates 1947 and its complex, bloody aftermath in historical, political and aesthetic terms. This original collection conceives of Indian independence in bold and innovative ways by moving across national boundaries and disciplinary, geopolitical and linguistic landscapes; and by examining a wealth of under-researched primary material, both recent and historical. *India at 70* is a unique and indispensable contribution to Indian history, literary and cultural studies.

Ruth Maxey is Associate Professor in Modern American Literature at the University of Nottingham. She is the author of *South Asian Atlantic Literature, 1970–2010* (2012) and *Understanding Bharati Mukherjee* (2019).

Paul McGarr is Associate Professor in US Foreign Policy at the University of Nottingham and author of *The Cold War in South Asia, 1945–1965* (2013). He is currently writing a book on the history of Anglo-American secret intelligence and security interventions in India and Pakistan.

Routledge Studies in Modern History
https://www.routledge.com/history/series/MODHIST

53 Model Workers in China, 1949–1965
Constructing A New Citizen
James Farley

54 Making Sense of Mining History
Themes and Agendas
Edited by Stefan Berger and Peter Alexander

55 Transatlantic Trade and Global Cultural Transfers Since 1492
More Than Commodities
Edited by Martina Kaller and Frank Jacob

56 Contesting the Origins of the First World War
An Historiographical Argument
Troy R E Paddock

57 India at 70
Multidisciplinary Approaches
Edited by Ruth Maxey and Paul McGarr

58 1917 and the Consequences
Edited by Gerhard Besier and Katarzyna Stoklosa

59 Reforming Senates
Upper Legislative Houses in North Atlantic Small Powers 1800–present
Edited by Nikolaj Bijleveld, Colin Grittner, David E. Smith and Wybren Verstegen

60 Unsettled 1968 in the Troubled Present
Revisiting the 50 Years of Discussions from East and Central Europe
Edited by Aleksandra Konarzewska, Anna Nakai and Michal Przeperski

61 Marginalized Groups, Inequalities and the Post-War Welfare State
Whose Welfare?
Edited by Monika Baár and Paul van Trigt

For a full list of titles, please visit: https://www.routledge.com/history/series/MODHIST

India at 70
Multidisciplinary Approaches

Edited by Ruth Maxey and Paul McGarr

LONDON AND NEW YORK

First published 2020
by Routledge
2 Park Square, Milton Park, Abingdon, Oxon OX14 4RN

and by Routledge
52 Vanderbilt Avenue, New York, NY 10017

Routledge is an imprint of the Taylor & Francis Group, an informa business

© 2020 selection and editorial matter, Ruth Maxey and Paul McGarr; individual chapters, the contributors

The right of Ruth Maxey and Paul McGarr to be identified as the authors of the editorial material, and of the authors for their individual chapters, has been asserted in accordance with sections 77 and 78 of the Copyright, Designs and Patents Act 1988.

All rights reserved. No part of this book may be reprinted or reproduced or utilised in any form or by any electronic, mechanical, or other means, now known or hereafter invented, including photocopying and recording, or in any information storage or retrieval system, without permission in writing from the publishers.

Trademark notice: Product or corporate names may be trademarks or registered trademarks, and are used only for identification and explanation without intent to infringe.

British Library Cataloguing-in-Publication Data
A catalogue record for this book is available from the British Library

Library of Congress Cataloging-in-Publication Data
A catalog record has been requested for this book

ISBN: 978-0-367-35499-2 (hbk)
ISBN: 978-0-429-33180-0 (ebk)

Typeset in Times
by Deanta Global Publishing Services, Chennai, India.

Contents

List of figures vii
List of contributors viii

Introduction: Framing India at 70 1
RUTH MAXEY AND PAUL MCGARR

PART I
Political and historical context: At home and abroad 13

1 The making of the *New Kashmir* manifesto 15
  ANDREW WHITEHEAD

2 Half-widows and the travesty of justice in
  Indian-administered Kashmir 33
  SOHINI CHATTERJEE

3 The RSS's 'Village Republics' 47
  RAKESH ANKIT

4 Cartooning politics: Reading the *Daily Mail*,
  Dawn and *Hindustan Times* 61
  NASSIF MUHAMMED ALI

PART II
Aesthetic responses to Indian modernity 77

5 The experience of the Left cultural movement in India:
  1942 to the present 79
  ARJUN GHOSH

6 Contested natures and tribal identities: Regional nationalism as ethnography – rereading Rajam Krishnan's *When the Kurinji Blooms* 92
ANITA BALAKRISHNAN

7 Material memory and the Partition of India: A narrative interview with Aanchal Malhotra 104
E. DAWSON VARUGHESE

8 Thinking gender in 21st-century India: Reflections on *Drawing the Line: Indian Women Fight Back* 117
SUKESHI KAMRA

Index 131

Figures

4.1	Indelible Writing on the Wall. Cartoon by Enver Ahmed	63
4.2	Not Yet master, We Still Need Each Other. Cartoon by Enver Ahmed	64
4.3	Loaves and Fishes. Cartoon by Enver Ahmed	65
4.4	Congress Retrievers. Cartoon by Enver Ahmed	65
4.5	Blitzkrieg. Cartoon by Shankar, *Hindustan Times*	70
4.6	Congrophobia. Cartoon by Shankar	71
4.7	Nothing Doing. Cartoon by Shankar	71
4.8	The Parity Business. Cartoon by Shankar	72
7.1	'The Pearls of Azra Haq' © Aanchal Malhotra	107
7.2	'Nazmuddin Khan seated outside his home in Hauz Rani, New Delhi, 2014' © Aanchal Malhotra	110
7.3	'Aanchal Malhotra interviewing Uma Sondhi Ahmad at her home in Kolkata, 2018' © Karuna Ezara Parikh	112
7.4	'The Dialect of Stitches and Secrets: The *Bagh* of Hansla Chowdhary' © Aanchal Malhotra	114
7.5	'Stones from My Soil: The *Maang-Tikka* of Bhag Malhotra' © Aanchal Malhotra	115

Contributors

Nassif Muhammed Ali is a PhD scholar at the Centre for Historical Studies, Jawaharlal Nehru University, New Delhi. He is working on the cartooning history in Malayalam in its formative four decades, viz. 1920–1960, through a set of five humour-based magazines: *Vidooshakan, Sanjayan, Vishwaroopam, Naradar* and *Sarasan*. His research interests include visual culture, modern Indian history, Partition and Indian independence, humour, humorous magazines, political cartoons and comic strips.

Rakesh Ankit is Lecturer in History at Loughborough University. He studied in Delhi, Oxford and Southampton and has taught at Jindal University, Sonipat. He is author of *The Kashmir Conflict: From Empire to Cold War, 1945–66* (2016) and *India in the Interregnum: Interim Government, September 1946–August 1947* (2019).

Anita Balakrishnan is Associate Professor in English at Queen Mary's College, Chennai, India. She has an MPhil and PhD from the University of Madras, Chennai. Her doctoral work was on the revitalisation of the *Bildungsroman* form by American ethnic women writers. She has been published widely both nationally and internationally in journals such as *South Asian Review* and *Language in India*. She has contributed an entry on Rabindranath Tagore to the *Wiley-Blackwell Encyclopedia of Postcolonial Studies* (2016). She has also contributed chapters to more than 20 books. She has edited *Transforming Spirit of Contemporary Indian Women Writers* (2012).

Sohini Chatterjee is an independent feminist researcher, whose work explores the intersections of gender, security and violence, primarily focused on postcolonial India's relationship with its borderlands. Chatterjee holds an MA in International Relations (IR) from South Asian University, New Delhi and is one of the editors of *HYSTERIA*, a radical feminist periodical and activist platform. Her research interests are cross-disciplinary, traversing politics and gender and sexuality studies which have often led her to go beyond her disciplinary training in IR to nurture intellectual curiosities pertaining to feminist resistance movements, questions of gender, race and sexuality, and the politics of representation tied to them.

Contributors ix

E. Dawson Varughese is a scholar whose work examines the encoding of Indian post-millennial modernity through popular literary and (visual) artistic expression. She publishes on genre fiction, graphic narratives, domestic Indian book cover design and public wall art; a central theme to her research is (evolving) ideas of Indian-ness. Her most recent book is entitled *Visuality and Identity in Post-Millennial Indian Graphic Narratives* (2017). An independent scholar, she divides her time between the UK and India and she is a Senior Fellow at Manipal Centre of Humanities, South India. See her work at www.beyondthepostcolonial.com and www.seeingnewindia.com.

Arjun Ghosh is Associate Professor, Literature, at the Indian Institute of Technology Delhi. He works on the politics of performance and mobilisation, copyright and intellectual property, new media and the internet. He was formerly a Fellow at the Indian Institute of Advanced Study, Shimla. He is the author of *A History of the Jana Natya Manch: Plays for the People* (2012), *Freedom from Profit: Eschewing Copyright in Resistance Art* (2014) and an annotated translation of *Nabanna* (2018).

Sukeshi Kamra is Professor in the Department of English Language and Literature at Carleton University, Ottawa, Canada. Her research and teaching interests include contemporary Anglophone Indian literature, postcolonial theory, law and the Indian press of British India, revolutionary nationalism, and the 1947 Partition of India. She has written books and articles on all these subjects.

Aanchal Malhotra is an award-winning oral historian and author of *Remnants of a Separation: History of the Partition through Material Memory* (2017), published in the UK under the title *Partition: 21 Objects from a Continent Divided* (2019). She is also the co-founder of the Museum of Material Memory, a digital repository tracing family histories and social ethnography through heirlooms, collectibles and antiques from the Indian subcontinent. She lives in New Delhi, and more of her work can be seen on www.aanchalmalhotra.com.

Ruth Maxey is Associate Professor in Modern American Literature at the University of Nottingham. She is the author of *South Asian Atlantic Literature, 1970–2010* (2012) and *Understanding Bharati Mukherjee* (2019).

Paul McGarr is Associate Professor in US Foreign Policy at the University of Nottingham and author of *The Cold War in South Asia, 1945–1965* (2013). He is currently writing a book on the history of Anglo-American secret intelligence and security interventions in India and Pakistan.

Andrew Whitehead is Honorary Professor at the University of Nottingham and the author of *A Mission in Kashmir* (2007) and *The Lives of Freda: The Political, Spiritual and Personal Journeys of Freda Bedi* (2019). He has a longstanding association with *History Workshop Journal*, currently as an Associate Editor. He is a former BBC India correspondent and in a long career with the BBC was also the Editor of BBC World Service News. He has established an oral history archive related to Partition, which is held at SOAS, University of London.

Introduction
Framing India at 70

Ruth Maxey and Paul McGarr

On 15 August 2017, India's prime minister, Narendra Modi, delivered his fourth independence-day address from the ramparts of old Delhi's historic Red Fort. As excited crowds waving the Indian tricolour thronged the streets of the national capital, Modi chose the 70th anniversary of the nation's independence from British colonial rule to issue a rallying cry for national unity and collective action. Evoking the spirit of activism and resolve that had secured India its freedom back in 1947, Modi called on his fellow citizens to set aside their differences, and work to eradicate the social ills of communalism, casteism, corruption and poverty, and confront the security threat posed by terrorism.

But, in a speech heavily laden with symbolism, was Modi correct in stating that, under his governance, India had benefited from peace, harmony and unity? Did the vision of inclusivity, tolerance, modernity and development conjured up by India's controversial premier accurately reflect the state of the nation after seven decades of self-governance?

Many commentators regard India's post-independence history as chequered. The story of India has been largely one of democratic statehood and economic development. Such compelling narratives have, however, frequently masked the complexities of the national landscape from which they emerged: a landscape confronting not only fissiparous regional, linguistic and communal pressures, but also increasingly shaped by the broader international currents of globalisation and a communications revolution. India today – with Modi as a prime minister promoting Hindu nationalism, or *Hindutva*, as a panacea for the purported inadequacies of a traditionally more liberal, secular and heterogeneous political culture – remains mired in social and religious tensions at home and, in the form of Pakistan and China, faces seemingly perennial national security threats along its borders.

India's emergence as an independent sovereign state set in train an extended, and continuing, process of political, social, economic and cultural transformation. Defining the country's political character and cultural identity has proved challenging. *India at 70: Multidisciplinary Approaches* examines the influence exercised by differing ideas about socio-political and aesthetic organisation in the context of individuals intimately involved in the nation's post-independence history. It brings together the most recent research from early-career academics and established commentators pioneering new approaches to reimagining contemporary India. This volume argues for a common reading of Indian political and cultural development, interpreting each not as an insular, exclusive phenomenon, but rather as part of connected, if occasionally incongruous, agents of social transformation. It contributes to a burgeoning corpus of work that privileges the reciprocity of political and cultural milestones in the story of India, from the subcontinent's partition to the ongoing process of economic liberalisation, and that determines to make sense of these intersections in a variety of ways (see, for example, Khilnani, 2016; Guha, 2017; and Sen, 2005).

Political and historical context: At home and abroad

Contemporary India is beset with enervating problems of poverty and inequality. At the same time, the country is commonly lauded as a rising regional and global power. Its status as the world's largest democracy has led many commentators to characterise India as crucial to the future stability of Asia, and the wider international system (Gordon, 2014). Challenged by an exceptional range of social and religious diversity, a political plurality that has spawned hundreds of representative parties, and pressing internal and external security concerns, India's vibrant democracy is in many ways a testament to the enduring resilience and optimism of its citizens. Economically, having weathered decades of stultifying fiscal growth occasioned by a slavish adherence to state-centric development, India has come to embrace liberal capitalism. While of late the Indian economy has begun to outpace China's, such growth has come at a heavy environmental cost and has led to rising wealth inequality (Crabtree, 2018).

Equally, as traditionally marginalised and disadvantaged groups, from Dalits to women, have achieved notable successes in advancing universal political and economic justice and enhancing social mobility, others, and most especially India's Muslims (as Rakesh Ankit's contribution to this volume makes plain), continue to feel vulnerable and excluded. Moreover, India's socio-economic tensions have played out against a backdrop of seemingly perennial security threats. A border dispute with China, that has rumbled on since the late 1950s, continues to sour New Delhi's relations with Beijing, and manifests in periodic bouts of mutual sabre-rattling. Above all, however, the vexed issue of Kashmir, and its toxic impact on India's relationship with Pakistan, remains the dominant leitmotif of contemporary South Asian security discourse, as it has since the subcontinent's partition in 1947 (Schofield, 1996; Bose, 2009). In February 2019, the Pulwama attack on India's security forces in Jammu and Kashmir and, with Indian national elections looming, the Modi government's subsequent decision to abandon strategic restraint and launch retaliatory strikes into Pakistan, reignited concern over the wider international consequences of a conflagration between South Asia's nuclear neighbours.

Perhaps, however, the most urgent issue confronting India at 70 is how to reconcile a nationalist and parochial political turn with the wider global ambition that has accompanied the nation's accumulation of strategic, economic and cultural power. Modi has proved to be an effective communicator and a shrewd politician. Since he assumed office in May 2014, he has also presided over a government supported by militant Hindus who excuse and seek to legitimise violence directed at 'others' and, above all, India's Muslims. Notably, the close relationship between Modi's Bharatiya Janata Party (BJP), or Indian People's Party, and the Rashtriya Swayamsevak Sangh (RSS), a Hindu fundamentalist organisation and primary political patron of the BJP, has called into question India's continuing commitment to secularism and social pluralism. In a wider context, Modi's reluctance to speak out against high-profile cases of communalism and other forms of discrimination in India risks derailing his government's designs for the nation to play a bigger role on the world stage. Recent American presidents, the European Union and other key players in the international community have acknowledged India's rising importance and sought to build bridges with Modi's administration. Still, back in February 2002, Modi's association with communal violence in the western state of Gujarat left over 1000 Indians, chiefly Muslim, dead. This led Washington to deny him a US visa. International support for Modi, his BJP government and, ultimately, India, remains contingent on its capacity to ensure there is no repetition of the events of 2002.

Aesthetic responses to Indian modernity

How does art – literature, cinema, visual culture and music – respond to Indian modernity? Specifically, how have artists represented the nation through these different forms in the decades leading up to 2017 and the 70th anniversary of independence from British imperial rule? How can individual works of art navigate the creative challenges of reflecting such a complex, diverse, immense nation, composed of so many languages, religions and ethnicities? These are perennial, fraught, stimulating questions for Indian artists which can be instructively explored through specific cinematic and literary works produced since 1947.

Much contemporary Indian literature and film is concerned with the rise of India in the 21st century; tradition versus modernity; sexual, religious and gendered oppression; the place of minority groups; and the recovery of hidden histories. One aesthetic examination of this tension between ancient and modern, released in the 70th year of Indian independence, is Shubhashish Bhutiani's first feature film, the Hindi-language *Mukti Bhawan* (*Hotel Salvation*, 2017). Both dreamlike and socially realist, it is an intimate observation of close family relationships – domestic, gently comic, touching and ultimately optimistic – deploying a combination of convincing dialogue and the power of what is left unsaid. Modernity is represented through smartphones and communication through Skype; the particular professional pressures faced by the protagonist Rajiv; and his daughter Sunita's refusal of the groom Rajiv has selected for her in favour of a new job. The film privileges Hindu tradition and ritual through its use of Varanasi, a world-famous city and sacred setting. *Hotel Salvation* explores patrilineage and Rajiv's complex feelings of love, loyalty and respect, but also anger and resentment, towards his father Dayanand. It is also about the close bond between a grandfather and granddaughter with Dayanand appearing to understand Sunita better than her father does and embracing feminism more than Rajiv seems willing to do.

The relationship between Dayanand and Rajiv and their stay in Varanasi act as the film's main framing device. This recalls both Indian and European intertexts from Satyajit Ray's Bengali classic *Aparajito* (1956) to Ismaël Ferroukhi's French-language movie *Le Grand Voyage* (*The Great Journey*, 2004) in which a French Moroccan father and son rebuild their relationship through a pilgrimage to Mecca. The scenes in Rajiv's office recall the generic workplaces of such earlier films as Billy Wilder's *The Apartment* (1960, English) and Ritesh Batra's Hindi comedy-drama *The Lunchbox* (2013).[1] But the nature of Rajiv's work is not the point of Bhutiani's film: indeed, its unspecified nature – like the namelessness of Rajiv's town – makes the story more wide-ranging, broadening the appeal of *Mukti Bhawan* through a blend of cultural specificity and universality. This is an ostensibly timeless family drama about life and death, yet it also pays clear attention to contemporary India with characters both respecting ancient religious rites and breaking with tradition.

Through the visual language of overhead shots and Rajiv's positioning at several moments in the film – whether looking through a grille or doorway or standing behind a curtain – Bhutiani accentuates his protagonist's sense of separation and distance in Varanasi: his status as an outsider and questioning observer. In this respect, and in Rajiv's reactions to the sensory experience of Varanasi in a film about the sheer reality of death, he stands in for the audience, mirroring their bid to make sense of 'India at 70' and the paradoxes of this sacred city. But whereas being in Varanasi brings out Rajiv's barely suppressed fear and guilt, the city appears to liberate his father. The longer Dayanand stays in Varanasi, the more vibrant and subversive he becomes, while Rajiv is forced to live at a different pace and understand his father better. These ideas and shifts are underscored by Tajdar Junaid's soundtrack which offers subtle, unobtrusive, emotionally suggestive music, highlighting moments of tension, mystery, suspense and uncertainty.

Turning specifically to Indian literature in English and the global appetite for fiction in particular, India remains a key topos in prize-winning Anglophone fiction. Contemporary novels about India can provide a crucial discursive and imaginative entry into the bewildering complexity and diversity of the modern nation. Recalling the international prominence of such bestselling fictions of India as Ruth Prawer Jhabvala's *Heat and Dust* (1975), Paul Scott's *Staying On* (1977), Salman Rushdie's *Midnight's Children* (1981), Arundhati Roy's *The God of Small Things* (1997), Kiran Desai's *The Inheritance of Loss* (2006) and Aravind Adiga's *The White Tiger* (2008) – all recipients of the illustrious, if controversial, Booker/Man Booker Prize – other recent, critically acclaimed English-language novels about India include Anjali Joseph's *Saraswati Park* (2010) and Kishwar Desai's *Witness the Night* (2010). The reception of these markedly different novels reflects the ongoing popularity and global kudos of Indian fiction in English, even as this body of writing continues to attract controversies about cultural appropriation and 'inauthenticity', especially when it is produced by diasporic authors (see Mendes, 2010).

Anticipating the themes of *Mukti Bhawan*, *Saraswati Park* also examines the tension between modernity and tradition. But Joseph offers a different male dyad, paralleling the story of Ashish, a young gay man coming of age on a visit to Mumbai, with that of Mohan, his emotionally withdrawn uncle, whose very profession as a letter-writer signals the analogue era and a vanishing way of life in India. This work has rendered Mohan semi-obsolete in contemporary India – and emotionally voiceless: 'he imagined writing her [his wife Lakshmi] a letter ... He, who'd turned others' feelings and concerns into more shapely phrases for years, couldn't envisage words fixing anything here' (Joseph, 2010, 203). Mohan's role as a ghostwriter for others also belongs to Joseph's wider interest in books and writing and her explicit use of intertextuality. Hence a wealth of Indian and European works are cited by name: from the *Bhagavad Gita*, the *Upanishads*, and Amit Chaudhuri's novel *A New World* (2000), which *Saraswati Park* echoes in its gently satirical, domestic focus, to Shakespeare's *Romeo and Juliet* (1595) and Henry James's *The Ambassadors* (1903) and a French cinematic canon containing such thematically resonant works as Jean Cocteau's *La Belle et La Bête* (1946) and François Truffaut's *The 400 Blows* (1959). Mohan's inability to articulate his emotions reflects Joseph's thematic interest in her characters' inner lives: specifically, their secrets and withholding of information. Hence, in exploring the dangers and (then) illegality of a gay relationship through Ashish's involvement with Narayan, the secretive older man's first name is never given. This device, further suggested when he is simply called 'the teacher' (Joseph, 2010, 206), emphasises the distance in years and status between them. Joseph also maps Mumbai in the novel. Although the city is figured through images of poverty and squalor, Mumbai is a source of knowledge through the possibilities for personal growth and adventure it offers Ashish. And even though 'Saraswati Park' becomes a byword for understatement, underachievement and middle-class mediocrity, Saraswati is the Hindu goddess of wisdom, a modicum of which both Ashish and Mohan have achieved by the close of the novel.

By contrast, *Witness the Night* tackles 21st-century India in radically different fashion. Desai's suspenseful, page-turning, elegiac narrative condemns sexual violence against women and misogynistic societal expectations of girls; the widespread practice of people trafficking; and the lack of adequate mental healthcare in many parts of India. In this angry and shocking protest novel, Desai memorialises the victims of female infanticide, bearing witness to the many lost girls of India. She also stages a rescue fantasy whereby one woman, the Punjabi social worker Simran Singh, tries to liberate traumatised girls and women. This is a polyphonic novel of female voices where Simran's first-person account is interspersed with those of Durga, an abused girl, and Brinda/Binny, Durga's sister-in-law. Desai makes these deeply troubling themes more accessible by fictionalising them, yet her novel is also strongly exophoric, as shown in the 'Author's Note'. Here she is keen to point out that

> while the characters and places in this book are entirely fictional, the events which take place are not. There is a complicity of corruption between the police ... judicial system, politicians, media and the uncivil society ... gender issues are still treated with contempt.
>
> (Desai, 2010, 275)

This was before the 2012 *cause célèbre* of Jyoti Singh, discussed in Chapter 8 of this book, but the issues behind Desai's claims remain as pressing and pertinent as ever.

Volume organisation

India at 70 suggests several important areas for interrogating recent Indian history, contemporary politics, literature and visual culture, without claiming to represent an exhaustive or definitive analytical template. First, the volume draws attention to some of the latest innovations in critical thinking that can assist in uncovering elided connections between political discourse and cultural production; second, it underlines the value in incorporating new and interdisciplinary perspectives into the study of modern Indian history and contemporary culture. At its heart, this approach necessitates posing different and challenging sets of research questions, but in addition it also requires that more familiar problems are considered from unorthodox viewpoints. *India at 70* does not constitute an exhaustive examination of either the recent history of Indian politics or the nation's cultural capital, or, for that matter, their many interactions. The chapters featured are not intended to present a systematic and seamless picture of Indian progression, but instead in many instances to highlight divergent thinking and productive critical disjunctures that have developed between scholars and commentators on material issues. We have purposely included chapters from contributors that employ different methodologies and draw different conclusions on common themes.

The volume begins with a section that explores the historical and political context of Indian nationalism, ideology and state formation as postcolonial projects. One means of questioning tensions inherent in balancing stability and national security with individual freedoms and civil liberty, is to ponder how the ideological project of India as a modern, technocratic, egalitarian, and secular state or, as one prominent commentator has reflected, the 'idea of India' (Khilnani, 1997), has played out. Borrowing from Khilnani's formulation, this section spotlights the extent to which a chasm has grown between the idea of India, and an everyday lived reality experienced by many of its citizens. In its second section, the volume goes on to address artistic responses to contemporary India. Moving beyond a focus upon Partition and its legacy, the subject of a number of fine recent academic collections reflecting upon India since 1947 (see, for example, Butalia, 2015; and Jalil, Saint and Sengupta, 2017), the concluding section privileges the many other afterlives of Indian independence.

Past and present: Political and social landscapes

Part I of *India at 70* features contributions from historians and international relations experts that provide fresh perspectives on the enervating issue of Kashmir, innovative reinterpretations of the subcontinent's Partition through the visual prism of print culture, and penetrating analysis on enduring problems of post-independence Indian Muslim identity. Andrew Whitehead's opening chapter recovers the socio-political significance of the *New Kashmir* manifesto adopted by the main Kashmiri nationalist party, Sheikh Abdullah's National Conference, in 1944 (Chapter 1). The manifesto has been described as the most important political document in Kashmir's modern history. It was a hugely radical and ambitious draft constitution for the then princely-ruled state, incorporating charters for workers, peasants and women. Very few nationalist movements had developed such a detailed policy prescription at such an early date. *New Kashmir* gave notice of some of the measures which the National Conference implemented when, after 1947, it was the ruling party in what became the Indian state of Jammu and Kashmir: notably its advocacy of land redistribution under the slogan 'land to the tiller' and also in the provision of women's education. Whitehead probes the roots of the manifesto, and recognises the influential role taken in its drafting by a Punjabi Communist, B.P.L. Bedi, and his English wife, Freda Bedi. *New Kashmir* was largely written by members of the Communist Party of India, who looked to Soviet documents for inspiration. Whitehead demonstrates that, as one of the most important examples of the Communist left influencing radical but non-Communist nationalist parties in South Asia, *New Kashmir* posed searching questions about the formation of the new state's economy and systems of governance. Revisiting a struggle for Kashmir's political identity thus becomes a key marker for better understanding the contestations of India's broader political evolution.

The centrality of Kashmir to contemporary debates surrounding Indian identity is explored further by Sohini Chatterjee in her chapter on the state's 'half-widows' (Chapter 2), or women whose husbands have disappeared and whose fate remains unknown. In recent decades Kashmir has proved a hotbed of conflict and violence, leading to the production of different gendered identities and the proliferation of their associated vulnerabilities. Chatterjee's chapter emphasises that as a consequence of the specificities of their geographical location, as well as their social categorisation, the 'half-widows' of Kashmir have been both victims and survivors of violence. Illustrating the varieties of violence endured by women identified and identifying as 'half widows', Chatterjee elucidates how justice, in its economic, political and socio-cultural forms, has failed these individuals. Offering up a compelling account of the afterlives of the 1,500 'half-widows' resident in Indian-administered Kashmir, Chatterjee underscores how violence and justice remain inextricably linked within the troubled state.

Switching to an interrogation of the role played by communal politics in India's emergence as an independent sovereign state, Nassif Muhammed Ali's chapter utilises newspaper cartoons to provide imaginative new perspectives on the subcontinent's Partition (Chapter 4). Ali explores how the subcontinent's cartoonists have frequently illuminated points of domestic tension and sought to mediate national differences. Offering a close critical reading of cartoons published in a cross-section of newspapers, Ali revisits the causes and the consequences of the socio-political tumult that swept through South Asia in the period immediately before August 1947. At that time, demands for and against bifurcating India along religious lines dominated political discourse. Newspapers, as a medium that both influenced and reflected public opinion, turned increasingly partisan. Notably, *Dawn* and the *Pakistan Times* came to champion the Muslim League, while the *Hindustan Times* and *Tribune* promoted the Congress Party's line. Ali illustrates how such allegiances were reflected in the cartoons that newspapers published, which invariably evidenced a subtext and socio-political narrative that was often absent, or elided, in the printed word.

Bringing the issue of communal politics into the present, Rakesh Ankit's chapter explores challenges surrounding Muslim public prayer (Chapter 3). Ankit addresses the case of Devru, a small village located in Haryana, which has been characterised as 'another Ayodhya in the making'. In recent years, Devru has become synonymous with the emergence of a *Hindu Rashtra*, or Hindu polity, in north India. The Devru controversy centres on an old and dilapidated village mosque, and the plans for its conversion into a community hall by Hindu nationalist groups, abetted by the local police, media and judiciary. Ankit's chapter uses the case of Devru to unpick a wider and growing unease that surrounds Muslims as a 'political category' in India. Tracing the Devru story over the course of 50 years, Ankit contextualises its significance within the paradigm of 'incorporative violence': Muslims' fate in India. If the absence of physical violence signals normality, Ankit suggests, then the situation in Devru is 'normal'. However, for the village's Muslims, and many of their co-religionists across India, this constitutes a new and troubling development. Seventy years since 1947, Ankit postulates, Muslims are experiencing an afterlife as India's 'internal other'.

Old and new: Cultural and aesthetic interventions

In Part II of *India at 70*, key themes such as development, modernity, violence and nationalism remain, although our analysis turns to cultural and literary studies, focusing particularly on inventive approaches to Partition, environmentalism, memory and material culture. The section opens with a chapter by Arjun Ghosh arguing that the establishment of the Indian People's Theatre Association (IPTA) in 1942 marked a watershed moment in the history of Indian theatre, shaping aesthetics that broke free from colonial frames of reference and sought to represent the reality of poverty, both rural and urban, via indigenous cultural forms (Chapter 5). Yet there remained a contradiction between these proletarian goals and the middle-class background of the IPTA's leftist cultural activists, resulting in a conflict between the aesthetic and political goals of the organisation. Ghosh contends that, although the IPTA disintegrated rapidly after Indian independence, its aesthetic vision remained influential for several decades. Hence the Drama Seminar run by the Sangeet Natak Akademi in 1956 ruled that colonial European forms were incapable of representing Indian realities and called for the adoption of indigenous forms. But even though the aesthetic goals of the IPTA continued to sway theatrical practice, the Indian Left could not overcome the organisational contradictions that had led to the demise of the IPTA and, Ghosh demonstrates, it was not until the 1970s – around the movements against the imposition of Indira Gandhi's Emergency – that the Indian Left once again turned to cultural activists for solidarity and support. Examining left-wing intervention in Indian theatre since the 1940s, this chapter critically appraises questions surrounding the relationship between culture and organised politics in India.

Anita Balakrishnan's chapter charts the acute conflict arising from the growing disjuncture between territorial spaces inhabited by tribal people and the economic spaces occupied by development projects (Chapter 6). Arguing that regional writers depict a specific relationship to nature by claiming landscape as a place of origin, she focuses on the Tamil writer Rajam Krishnan, whose novel *Kurinjithen* (1996), published in English in 2002 as *When the Kurinji Blooms*, examines the impact of colonialist development on the distinctive culture and way of life of the Badaga tribe in the Nilgiris region of Tamil Nadu. Balakrishnan contends that Krishnan's ethnographic narrative allows two mutually exclusive discourses to cohabit: the recuperation of the oral histories, tribal rituals and everyday practices of the Badaga tribespeople and a simultaneous critique of the devastating impact on such customs arising from the construction of the Pykara Dam in the region. Hence Jogi, the protagonist, is rendered a subaltern, impoverished by the hegemony of the colonial state, illustrating that, as Ramachandra Guha and Joan Martinez Alier (1997) observe, industrial development in India has benefited only a tiny elite while exacting a huge social and environmental cost. Balakrishnan shows that in Krishnan's novel, the Badaga people may be marginalised by such development, yet this does not make them coalesce into an effective protest group. Rather, the forces of modernity serve to splinter the tribe into opposing factions who react variously to the ecological crisis. Balakrishnan's reading explores the ramifications of this crisis through the concept of 'ecological nationalism', whereby cultural and political aspirations are linked with programmes of natural conservation and environmental protection and expressed through the rhetoric of civil and human rights.

E. Dawson Varughese's chapter centres upon an interview conducted with Aanchal Malhotra, a multidisciplinary artist and oral historian. Malhotra's book, *Remnants of a Separation*, published in 2017, merges history and anthropology by exploring the role that material culture plays in moments of rupture and transition (Chapter 7). It asks about the functional use of objects – which 'practical' objects do you choose to take with you when you flee? – while also questioning how personal emotions and memories become embedded (and embodied) within such items. Varughese's interview with Malhotra considers how the 'object' of a material memory research study both leads and gives way to a certain kind of thinking, reminiscing and invocation of the past. Malhotra recalls the genesis of her research for *Remnants of a Separation* when, at her maternal grandparents' house in New Delhi in 2013, she encountered a *ghara* (metallic vessel) and *gaz* (yardstick) and grasped the importance of material memory in the retrieval of a familial past deeply affected by Partition. The interview reveals Malhotra's own bid to 'remember' Partition, a deeply traumatic event for her grandparents; her negotiation of the researcher–participant experience; and what this experience has afforded the author for her own life story.

The concluding chapter by Sukeshi Kamra examines *Drawing the Line* (2015), a recent collection of feminist graphic narratives by Indian women artists that tackles the lived experience of gendered, sexual, caste and communal violence (Chapter 8). Taking the gang rape of Jyoti Singh as a pivotal moment, even limit event, in Indian histories of violence, Kamra argues that this visual storytelling operates as testimony while questioning teleologies of Indian 'progress' and the sensationalist media coverage of public violence. She situates this collection within the wider context of Indian graphic narratives and the specific ways in which this form can challenge triumphalist visions of nationalism. Concluding with a brief consideration of *The Elephant in the Room: Women Draw Their World* (2018), Kamra observes that this new collection echoes *Drawing the Line* by revealing the complexity and multiplicity of creative perspectives at work within the Indian graphic narrative.

In summary, *India at 70* re-evaluates the agency exercised by both elite political actors and ordinary citizens as they have worked to fashion Indian society in a multitude of different ways, and with varying degrees of success. During the past 70 years, the idea of India, and the contrasting shades of rhetoric associated with it, has fed national anxieties and energised the country's political and cultural consciousness. In turn, a process of continuous, vibrant and occasionally tumultuous social, political and economic debate has occurred. Viewed in the round, this volume not only reflects on the interplay between Indian modernity, development, identity, and collective memory, but also reconsiders the salience and impact of each phenomenon. It represents an initial intervention in the process of unpacking India's journey from a fragile nascent post-colonial state to an assertive 21st-century powerhouse, suggesting specific ways in which ideology, religion, race and economics have influenced its citizens at all levels. Nonetheless, the idea of India remains an elusive concept resistant to easy categorisation, underlining the imperative of further interdisciplinary exchange in this area across ideological, regional, linguistic, thematic and methodological boundaries. In short, our aspiration is that *India at 70* will underscore the numerous directions in which the study of India and its historical and cultural influence is, and can continue, to flourish.

Note

1 Bhutiani's avowed influences here are Yasujiro Ozu (dir.), *Tokyo Story* (1953) and Wong-Kar Wai (dir.), *In the Mood for Love* (2000); see Walsh, 2017.

Works cited

Bose, Sumantra (2009). *Kashmir: Roots of Conflict, Paths to Peace*. Cambridge, MA: Harvard University Press.
Butalia, Urvashi (ed.) (2015). *Partition: The Long Shadow*. Delhi: Zubaan.

Crabtree, James (2018). *The Billionaire Raj: A Journey Through India's Gilded Age*. London: Oneworld.

Desai, Kishwar (2010). *Witness the Night*. London: Simon & Schuster.

Gordon, Sandy (2014). *India's Rise as an Asian Power: Nation, Neighborhood, and Region*. Washington, DC: Georgetown University Press.

Guha, Ramachandra (2017). *India after Gandhi: The History of the World's Largest Democracy*. Delhi: Macmillan.

Guha, Ramachandra, and Joan Martinez Alier (1997). *Varieties of Environmentalism: Essays from North and South*. New Delhi: Oxford University Press.

Jalil, Rakhshanda, Tarun K. Saint and Debjani Sengupta (eds.) (2017). *Looking Back: The 1947 Partition of India 70 Years On*. Telangana: Orient Blackswan.

Joseph, Anjali (2010). *Saraswati Park*. London: Fourth Estate.

Khilnani, Sunil (1997). *The Idea of India*. London: Hamish Hamilton.

Khilnani, Sunil (2016). *Incarnations: India in 50 Lives*. London: Allen Lane.

Mendes, Ana Cristina (2010). 'Exciting Tales of Exotic Dark India: Aravind Adiga's *The White Tiger*'. *Journal of Commonwealth Literature*, 45(2), 275–293.

Scofield, Victoria (1996). *Kashmir in Conflict: India, Pakistan and the Unending War*. London: I.B. Tauris.

Sen, Amartya (2005). *The Argumentative India: Writings on Indian History, Culture and Identity*. London: Allen Lane.

Walsh, Joseph (2017). 'Hotel Salvation Director: "I Like to Watch a Little Comedy Every Day. If I Didn't, How Would I Maintain Sanity?"' *BFI Film Forever*. 22 August. www.bfi.org.uk/news-opinion/news-bfi/interviews/hotel-salvation-shubhashish-bhutiani. Accessed 22 March 2019.

Part I
Political and historical context: At home and abroad

1 The making of the *New Kashmir* manifesto

Andrew Whitehead

In May 1949, India's then prime minister, Jawaharlal Nehru, wrote to his friend and ally Sheikh Abdullah, the prime minister of the state of Jammu and Kashmir, to warn about one of the Kashmiri leader's key advisors. B.P.L. Bedi, a Punjabi and a Communist, was an influential figure in Sheikh Abdullah's inner circle. Nehru wanted Bedi kept at a distance. He said that 'quite a number' of the embassies in the Indian capital 'are greatly worried at, what they say, [is] the Communist infiltration into Kashmir'.

> Most of them have heard about Bedi and they enquire about him. ... I have no personal grievance against Bedi, but in view of the trouble we are having with the Communist Party in India, naturally Bedi's name is constantly coming up before people here.
>
> (Nehru, 1978: 143)

Whatever Sheikh Abdullah's reply, Nehru wasn't satisfied and a few days later he wrote again:

> You referred to the Bedis. I rather like them and especially Freda. I know that Freda left the Communist Party some years ago. What she has done since, I don't know. But so far as I know, Bedi has continued in the Party, and the Party, especially today, does not tolerate any lukewarm people or those who do not fall in line with their present policy.
>
> I do not want you to push out the Bedis and cause immediate distress to them. But I do think that no responsible work should be given to them and they should be kept completely in the background.
>
> (Nehru, 1978: 149–151)

Nehru need not have worried. Kashmir's prime minister may not have taken kindly to advice from Delhi, but he was becoming disenchanted with the divided loyalties of his Communist supporters. B.P.L. Bedi's influence was on the wane in Srinagar and he was also increasingly out of step with the Communist Party of India (CPI), which had lurched towards an ultra-left policy of support for peasant insurrection. Within a few years, Bedi was out of Kashmir and out of the party.

Throughout the 1940s, B.P.L. Bedi and his English wife, Freda Bedi, were influential figures within Sheikh Abdullah's party, the National Conference. The party was the main standard-bearer of Kashmiri nationalism and an opponent of princely autocracy. B.P.L. Bedi performed a signal contribution to it: he put together the party's landmark statement of political purpose. This was not simply a collection of slogans and demands but a substantial forty-four page document, containing a proposed constitution for Jammu and Kashmir and a detailed economic plan. It was both a manifesto for the National Conference and a blueprint for Kashmir's future. Sheikh Abdullah spoke approvingly of this 'revolutionary' document and recounted how Bedi and other Communists came to his aid in compiling what became known as *Naya* or *New Kashmir*:

> To compile the manifesto we requisitioned the services of a famous progressive friend from Panjab [sic], B.P.L. Bedi. ... Bedi's sharp-minded, elegant wife Freda typed the manuscript. The manifesto completed, the concerned departments of the National Conference gave their approval to it.
> (Abdullah, 2013: 217–218)

New Kashmir stands out for the breadth of its ambition and the radicalism of the policies it espoused. The political scientist Sumantra Bose has described it as 'the most important political document in modern Kashmir's history' (Bose, 2009: 25–26). Few nationalist parties had ever sought to put together such a comprehensive statement of their political aims. When in October 1947 Sheikh Abdullah came to power in the Kashmir Valley, 'New Kashmir' was the name by which his project of modernising the former princely state became known. Some of its main provisions, particularly in agrarian and land reform, were acted upon. More broadly it marked out the National Conference as socialist in its political outlook – a progressive force in a corner of the subcontinent where there was little radical lineage – and distinguished the party from its politically and socially more conservative rival, the Muslim Conference.

This chapter seeks to retrieve something of B.P.L. Bedi's method in compiling *New Kashmir*, and his debt in particular to what is at first glance an unlikely model for a political dispensation in a princely state, much of which nestled in the foothills of the Himalayas. The source of inspiration for *New Kashmir* was the constitution for the Soviet Union adopted in December 1936 and generally known as the Stalin Constitution. The other key aspect of *New Kashmir*, the advocacy of far-reaching land redistribution, has a less clear derivation – though Bedi claimed this too as his handiwork. This chapter examines the enmeshing of the Bedis' political activity with the ebb and flow of progressive politics in Kashmir. It also traces B.P.L. Bedi's political role in Kashmir until, in the early 1950s, he broke with both Sheikh Abdullah and the Communist Party. Sheikh Abdullah himself became undone not long after. He was dismissed from office in August 1953 and detained on suspicion of working with other countries to revisit the state's hurried accession to India. It was another twenty-two years before Abdullah regained power in Jammu and Kashmir.

Baba Pyare Lal Bedi was born in 1909 in Punjab into what he described as a feudal family. He grew up in a village and the rural Punjabi idiom he picked up served him well in later life as a leader of the Communist-aligned peasants' movement. After attending Government College, Lahore, Bedi followed in his brother's footsteps to Oxford University, with the intention of sitting the exams for admission to the Indian Civil Service. He quickly forsook that ambition and became embroiled in both nationalist and Communist politics. He attended meetings of the Oxford Majlis, where Indian students gathered, and of the Communist October Club, where his physique – he had been a hammer-thrower and wrestler – was put to good use to discourage barrackers and gatecrashers.

Bedi was loud, gregarious and outgoing. His student girlfriend was the opposite: a little shy, but both inquisitive and stubbornly determined. Freda Houlston was from a conventional middle-class household in Derby in the English East Midlands and went to a girls' school where only a handful of leavers went on to university and then rarely to Oxford. She later described her student years as 'the opening of the gates of the world', a literal as well as a metaphorical truth (Whitehead, 2019). In spite of the initial disapproval of Freda's family, and disciplinary action by her college which Freda believed was straightforward racial discrimination, the couple married at Oxford Register Office in June 1933 just a few days after their final examinations. Freda was probably disappointed by her third-class honours; Bedi fared still worse, but his fourth-class honours – a sign of academic mediocrity – did not prevent him from enrolling for doctoral research in Berlin. Their romance was strengthened by intellectual collaboration, with Freda probably taking the lead. 'She was quieter; she was the disciplining force behind B.P.L.', recalled Pran Chopra, who was part of the same social circle in Lahore (Whitehead, 2007c). By the time the couple arrived in Bombay (now Mumbai) with their baby son in October 1934 they had co-edited for the left-wing publishing house Victor Gollancz three substantial volumes about contemporary India (Bedi, 1933–1934).

Freda's first footing on Indian soil was marked by a rigorous search of the couple and their luggage. 'We had been listed as "politicals" because of our activities in London, mild though they were', Freda recalled. 'And we were subjected to body searches … and even Ranga's little napkin was taken off and searched because they thought I might be carrying messages in it.' The British authorities were determined to prevent Communist and militant nationalist propaganda being smuggled into India. 'Even in Hitlerite Germany', B.P.L. lamented, 'the search was never so thorough as here' (Bedi, 1969). For Freda, it must have seemed as if from the moment of her arrival in India, she was seen by the Raj as suspect. It can only have reaffirmed her identification with India and her rejection of Empire and the indignities it imposed on those it ruled.

Once settled in Lahore, B.P.L. Bedi acted on an idea put forward by his doctoral supervisor in Berlin, Werner Sombart. With his wife's active support, Bedi established a serious-minded nationalist and progressive quarterly, *Contemporary India*. This was an ambitious venture. The quarterly survived for ten issues over 1935–1937, each consisting of 160 or more pages. B.P.L. Bedi named himself as the editor; Freda Bedi was the managing editor. Many of India's most renowned nationalist-minded academics served as contributing editors. The rising star on the radical wing of the Indian National Congress, Subhas Chandra Bose, was among the contributors. *Contemporary India*'s agenda included India's economic and financial prospects, the development of industry and the plight of its peasantry, demands for Congress to develop a more activist approach, and also issues relating to gender, caste and popular culture. Its scope was international as well as nationalist. Articles ranged across developments in Burma, Japan and Palestine, as well as Hitler's increasing grip on power in Germany and developments in Stalin's Russia. The penultimate issue published in full both the new Soviet constitution adopted towards the end of 1936 and Stalin's speech commending it.

From the late 1930s, the Bedis were part of an informal group of leftists and progressive intellectuals who spent much of the summer in the Kashmiri capital, Srinagar, away from the punishing heat of the Punjab plains. Among these were the progressive writer Mulk Raj Anand and two men who later became commanding figures in Indian cinema, Balraj Sahni and K.A. Abbas. When in Lahore, Kashmiri nationalists met – and sometimes stayed with – leading leftists in the city. Strong bonds of friendship and political affinity developed. The Communist Party of India saw a clear opportunity both to recruit in the Kashmir Valley and to shape the agenda of progressive nationalism there (Jan, 2006: 59–86; Whitehead, 2010: 141–168; Kanth, 2018). The Bedis were remarkably adept in winning over a small but talented group of young Kashmiris to the Communist cause (Taseer, 1986: 141, 175; Giyas-ud-Din, 1999: 53). The CPI was banned in Punjab province from the summer of 1934 for eight years – until Nazi Germany's attack on the Soviet Union prompted the international Communist movement to support what they had previously denounced as an imperialist war. The party achieved influence through the Congress Socialist Party, through front organisations of which the peasants' movement was among the most important, and through reform-minded non-Communist parties.

B.P.L. Bedi was detained for 15 months in a camp in the Rajasthan desert during the early part of the Second World War as the British sought to quarantine Communist activists who might have sought to sabotage military recruitment. Freda Bedi also spent three months in jail after courting arrest as part of Gandhi's campaign of opposition to India's conscription into the Allied side in the war. After their release, Kashmir became an increasing focus of their activity. Bedi recalled that he happened to be in Kashmir on 8 August 1942 when the Congress announced its Quit India campaign, a civil disobedience movement demanding an end to British rule. According to Bedi's own account, he persuaded Sheikh Abdullah and other leaders of the National Conference to keep some distance from the Congress campaign to avoid giving a pretext for their arrest. Most of the national leadership of the Congress spent the rest of the war behind bars. Sheikh Abdullah had built up a strong personal and political allegiance with Nehru and the enforced departure from the political scene of prominent Congress leaders may have prompted Abdullah to turn more to the Communists for guidance and support. In a sign of a new axis emerging in Kashmir, the National Conference conspicuously echoed Indian Communists in praising the Soviet Red Army and its resistance to Hitler's invading forces at a time when Congress refused to endorse the Allied side in the war.

Kashmir was a princely-ruled autocracy, and prior to the 1930s there were no political parties, no rights of political assembly and few local newspapers in the Kashmir Valley. Maharaja Hari Singh had in 1934, under British pressure, agreed to constitute a legislative assembly – but it was an advisory body, most of its members were nominated or held an official post and the franchise for elected seats was very restricted. Sheikh Abdullah was the commanding figure in Kashmiri politics from the early 1930s until his death in 1982 – though his career was interrupted by repeated incarceration in first Kashmiri and then Indian jails. The party he led was not the only political force with popular support and at times was probably not the dominant movement, but by 1947 it was certainly the most effective – and as far as can be judged, the most widely supported – in the Kashmir Valley. The National Conference is usually labelled as a Kashmiri nationalist party, reflecting its emphasis on representing the interests of all citizens of the princely state (though its particular focus was the Kashmir Valley rather than Jammu or Ladakh) and not simply its Muslim majority. The party also identified closely with Indian nationalism. By the early 1940s, the National Conference had positioned itself as a progressive force with an emphasis on representing the underprivileged and advocating representative democracy within a constitutional monarchy. The extent to which the party viewed Jammu and Kashmir – or indeed simply the Kashmiri-speaking areas of the state – as a nation in any juridical sense is opaque (Zutshi, 2003). It wasn't one of the most pressing issues facing Kashmiri public life – at least, not until late in 1947.

In 1943, Maharaja Hari Singh convened a commission to look at constitutional change in his princely state. The National Conference agreed to take the seats offered to it even though there was no expectation that the commission would usher in far-reaching reform. B.P.L. Bedi later recalled how, when a National Conference representative on the commission complained that it was getting nowhere and the party considered withdrawing, he urged an alternative course of action:

> So I said, "Withdrawing is alright; anybody can do it; but your glory would be if you give them an alternative, ready-made constitution ... It would be a positive withdrawal. Here you are holding all this constitutional enquiry. We do not want to be associated with this milk-and-water set up. This is what we want. Either grant us this or we walk out, and it will become a historic document, it will be your commitment to the people and it will be your battle cry." They were very happy about it and it was after that, that it came to be drafted on behalf of the National Conference, that New Kashmir document which was presented to the Commission.
>
> (Bedi, 1969)

Bedi's account, recorded 25 years after the event, may make him appear a more central actor in this political drama than was the case. But several key figures echo Sheikh Abdullah's recollection that Bedi played the commanding role in the drafting of *New Kashmir*.

It is striking that most of those who worked with Bedi on *New Kashmir* were non-Kashmiris (Dhar, 2004: 183). Just as the British Party for many years sought to guide and instruct Indian Communists, Punjabi leftists took the lead in establishing Communist influence in the Kashmir Valley. Sheikh Abdullah didn't seek to disguise the left-wing imprint on *New Kashmir*, which he described, with some justification, as 'the first ever endeavour of [its] kind in the subcontinent'.

> Comments are made sometimes about the impact of Communism on the document. One aspect of Communist ideology is that it sides internationally with labourers and oppressed people, a fact that the National Conference has always appreciated. It has illumined its conscience not only by the Russian revolution but also by the ideals of the French revolution. Indeed, we too favoured combining the Communist ideology with democracy and liberal humanism.
>
> (Abdullah, 2013: 217–218)

M.Y. Saraf – then a young activist in the National Conference – believed that B.P.L. and Freda Bedi 'had been assigned to Srinagar by the Central Politburo [of the CPI] in Bombay' (Saraf, 1977: 643). It is probable that B.P.L. Bedi was acting with the approval of the CPI leadership – and perhaps at the Party's instigation – but at provincial rather than national level. 'It was [the] Punjab Communist Party who drafted the thing ... It was actually a group of people, but mainly B.P.L. Bedi', recalled Pran Nath Jalali, then a teenage Communist in Srinagar – adding that 'there was not much drafting to be done' as *New Kashmir* was 'almost a carbon copy' of a document produced in Soviet Central Asia (Whitehead, 2007b: 2).

P.N. Jalali's chance remark prompted a protracted piece of historical detective work – an attempt to track down the document which was, according to his testimony, such an important source for the *New Kashmir* manifesto. His memory, it turned out, was broadly correct – though the document in question came not from the periphery of the Soviet Union but its epicentre. With hindsight, it should not have taken so long to locate the original. B.P.L. Bedi was more of an activist than an ideologue and given the task of drafting a constitution, it is simply common sense that he would turn to the constitution he admired most and knew best – the one published in his quarterly journal some years earlier. The key constitutional provisions of *New Kashmir* were not, in any event, being assembled in a post-revolutionary situation where they would shape a new political order. They were being offered as a political statement, an aspiration, rather than as an abiding work of jurisprudence.

Bedi and his colleagues looked to the Stalin constitution not just for general guidance but copied out large parts of it in a manner which entirely justified Jalali's talk of a 'carbon copy'. They must have had before them the issue of

Contemporary India containing the 1936 constitution or another identical version – there are some slight differences in translation, for example, from the text published as a cheap pamphlet by the Russia Today Society in London (*The Soviet Socialist Constitution*, 1937). There was, of course, an almost obscene disparity between the rights and democratic dispensation set out in Stalin's constitution and the terror then gripping the Soviet Union – but Communists worldwide were largely blind to this until Khrushchev's denunciation of Stalin in 1956.

Of the 50 clauses of the constitution proposed in *New Kashmir*, all but 8 bore the imprint of Stalin's constitution; 17 clauses, that is, 1-in-3, were closely modelled on the Soviet document. In some cases, the wording was similar rather than identical. Clause 16 of the *New Kashmir* constitution stated that work 'shall be an obligation and a matter of honour to all citizens capable of work', bearing a clear echo of article 12 of the Soviet Constitution which stated: 'Work ... is the obligation of each citizen capable of working'. On other occasions, the wording was a precise copy: in the lengthy clause 23 of the constitution in *New Kashmir* specifying the jurisdiction of the National Assembly, for instance, many of the 22 listed responsibilities were reproduced exactly from a similar list, again with 22 subclauses, in article 14 of the Soviet document. The wholesale rifling of the Soviet document was extraordinary in its scale – and there was no direct or indirect acknowledgement of the inspiration provided by the Stalin constitution.

As for the contents of *New Kashmir*, a brief preamble to the proposed constitution declared, in poetic style, that its purpose was

> to raise ourselves and our children forever from the abyss of oppression and poverty, degradation and superstition, from medieval darkness and ignorance into the sunlit valleys of plenty ruled by freedom, science and honest toil, in worthy participation of the historic resurgence of the people of the East.

This impassioned rhetoric was complemented by the more workaday language of the clauses of the constitution. These specified equal rights regardless of nationality, religion, race or birth, as well as freedom of conscience and worship, freedom of speech and of the press and freedom of assembly and meeting. This was coupled with the right, indeed obligation, to work; and the right to bear arms was twinned with the obligation of universal compulsory military service. A National Assembly and system of local *panchayats* (councils) was to be elected 'on the basis of universal equal direct suffrage by secret ballot', with all aged 18 and over eligible to vote. The document specified the provision of free and universal compulsory education conducted in the mother tongue, while Urdu was to be the *lingua franca* of the state.

There were a few striking differences between the Soviet and Kashmiri documents which point to the markedly different contexts from which they arose. *New Kashmir* envisaged a constitutional monarchy, where the maharaja had democratic responsibilities but also retained the right to declare a mobilisation of the armed forces. The draft constitution set down that the jurisdiction of the National Assembly should be subject to 'the general control of the Maharaja', which was consistent with the established approach of the National Conference to seek 'a democratic and responsible government under the general aegis of the Maharaja' (Jan, 2006: 24). Within another two years, the National Conference had articulated a rejection of the treaty rights and acquisition on which princely rule – particularly in the Kashmir Valley – was based. The Quit Kashmir agitation launched by the National Conference in 1946 – an echo of the Congress's anti-British Quit India campaign of a few years earlier – was directed specifically against the Dogra dynasty, a Hindu princely family whose heartlands were in Jammu rather than in Kashmir. This mass campaign resulted in the arrest and trial of Sheikh Abdullah and many of his colleagues.

There were key omissions from the Soviet document as well as additions. The Stalin constitution gave expression to the leading role of the Communist Party, 'the vanguard of the toilers in their struggle for strengthening and developing the socialist system ... which represents the leading nucleus of all organisations of the toilers, both public and state'. There was no echo of this in the Kashmiri manifesto. Indeed clause four in *New Kashmir* which asserted the right to combine and organise differed from the Soviet document by stipulating the right of citizens to form political parties. There were limits to how much Bedi and his colleagues could – or wished to – borrow from the Soviet model.

There was also what, with hindsight, appears to be a strange omission in the draft constitution for Kashmir. Nowhere was there a discussion of accession – the issue at the heart of the Kashmir conflict, which has rumbled on from late 1947 until the present day. There was no mention at all of Pakistan (not then in existence, of course, but an aspiration of Jinnah's Muslim League) and only passing references to India. Both the National Conference and the rival Muslim Conference, Idrees Kanth has argued, 'were not exactly coherent in how they anticipated Kashmir's future political relationship with either India or Pakistan, or otherwise' (Kanth, 2018: 41).

The working assumption of *New Kashmir* was that Jammu and Kashmir would remain a separate state, and it put forward – in its proposed constitution and the accompanying economic plan – a series of initiatives and institutions which presupposed a national identity: a National Assembly and 'a completely democratic National government', a National Planning Commission, a National Agricultural Council and a National Educational Council tasked to set up a National University. This wasn't so much an assertion of Jammu and Kashmir's desire for independence as a statement that the National Conference – as its name suggests – saw Kashmir as a nation and that its ambitions were limited to the areas under the authority of the maharaja. The issue of accession which has blighted and divided the one-time princely state for more than seventy years was, in 1944, not a topic of political debate. Even towards the close of September 1947, six weeks after India and Pakistan gained independence, when Sheikh Abdullah was released from the maharaja's jail, he urged that Kashmir should achieve responsible government before it considered the issue of accession. It was the invasion of the state by tribal forces from Pakistan in late October 1947 – an informal armed force enjoying the support of sections of Pakistan's new leadership – which served as a political catalyst. That prompted the maharaja's flight from the Kashmir Valley to Jammu and his hurried accession to India. By the time the armed tribesmen had reached the outskirts of Srinagar, the maharaja had been eclipsed by Sheikh Abdullah, whom he had been obliged to appoint as emergency administrator. The Kashmiri nationalist leader had both popular support in the Valley and the confidence of the Indian government, whose troops succeeding in repulsing the invaders (Whitehead, 2007a).

The introduction to *New Kashmir* was, as P.N. Jalali remembered it, the only part of the document that required writing; and while in Sheikh Abdullah's name, it was drafted on his behalf. It opened with a quote – without attribution – from the Soviet writer, Ilya Ehrenburg: 'every new generation has received the torch [of progress] from the bleeding hands of men of thought and light. Today this torch is firmly grasped in our hands' (Gangulee, 1943). In grandiose language, Sheikh Abdullah then described the fight in which the National Conference was engaged. 'It is for the poor, against those who exploit them; for the toiling people of our beautiful homeland against the heartless ranks of the socially privileged.' Woven in to Sheikh Abdullah's heroic account of the growth and activities of the National Conference was a passage of purple pro-Soviet prose:

> The inspiring picture of the regeneration of all the different nationalities and peoples of the U.S.S.R., and their welding together into the united mighty Soviet State that is throwing back its barbarous invaders with deathless heroism, is an unanswerable argument for the building of democracy on the cornerstone of economic equality.
>
> (*New Kashmir*, 1944)

It reads as if an extract from a Soviet propaganda sheet – which, considering the manner in which *New Kashmir* was assembled, it might well have been.

The introduction, publishers' note, preamble and draft constitution took up eighteen pages of *New Kashmir* as it was published in English. The larger part of the document put forward a detailed national economic plan encompassing industry, handicrafts and agriculture and including charters of rights for peasants, workers and women. The tone of this section of *New Kashmir* was very different from the constitutional clauses – it reads much more as a campaigning document. The ideal of the National Conference was expressed as 'all-in democracy and all-out planning'. Professor K.T. Shah – the secretary of the Indian National Planning Commission established by Nehru – was quoted as advocating the central importance of planning. This reference to Shah, one of only two contemporary figures mentioned by name in the document, is a further indication of B.P.L. Bedi's imprint. K.T. Shah had been a contributor to *India Analysed*, the three volumes edited jointly by B.P.L. and Freda Bedi and published by Gollancz. He had welcomed the Bedis off the boat at Bombay and hosted the family on their first night together on Indian soil, and became a contributing editor to *Contemporary India*. He was later a member of India's Constituent Assembly – in which he contributed to the discussions on Kashmir (Rai, 2018: 201–221) – and the left-wing runner-up in India's first presidential election.

The *New Kashmir* economic plan advocated, in addition to a planned economy, the abolition of 'the big private capitalist'; all 'key' industries were to be 'managed and owned by the Democratic State of Jammu and Kashmir'. In an overwhelmingly rural state, the most important aspect of the economic document was its provisions for agriculture. The main goals, *New Kashmir* declared, were 'the organisation of agriculture on a more modern and rational footing and the provision for the peasant of a higher standard of living'. The basic principles were to be the 'abolition of landlordism', the provision of 'land to the tiller' and cooperative association in the production and sale of crops. There was no detailed policy proposal – no stipulation of a ceiling for land ownership or whether landlords would be compensated – but in what was still a semi-feudal state, this huge proposed transfer of land (and so of wealth and power) from the privileged to the peasantry portended a far-reaching social revolution.

'Land to the tiller' was the most resonant of the political slogans proclaimed by *New Kashmir*. It appears to have been first used by Chinese nationalists in the 1920s and became part of Indian political discourse in the following decade. Both Congress and the Communists made much use of the call in their post-independence land reform plans – which indicates how imprecise this demand was – but Sheikh Abdullah was arguably the first significant political leader to be associated with the policy of 'land to the tiller'. *New Kashmir* also contained a peasants' charter which reinforced the importance given to far-reaching land reform. 'All land which at present belongs to the landlords will revert to the peasant', it declared, while envisaging the abolition of all feudal dues and measures to make the peasant 'completely debt-free'.

B.P.L. Bedi remarked that land reform proposed in *New Kashmir* was 'a hundred per cent Communist program, incorporating the peasant program which we had with the All India Kisan Sabha' (Bedi, 1969). Bedi had been an important figure in the establishment of the Communist-led peasants' movement in Punjab and recalled that Sheikh Abdullah had been a 'distinguished visitor' at an early Kisan Sabha rally. *Contemporary India* published the manifesto adopted in 1936 at an All India Kisan Congress. This had demands – including the abolition of landlordism – similar to those included in *New Kashmir*, but it was not a precise model in scope or wording. Nor can any direct lineage be established with other early peasants' charters, manifestos and resolutions of the Kisan Sabha (Singh Surjeet, 1995). In particular the resonant phrase 'land to the tiller' – which came to be so emblematic of the peasants' movement – didn't appear in these early Kisan Sabha documents.

The National Conference's commitment to redistributing land to those who worked it was the most transformative of the initiatives pursued by Sheikh Abdullah and his colleagues when they came to power. In the course of 1948, while Indian and Pakistani armies were at war over Kashmir, the state's new rulers started work on a far-reaching programme of land reform. Two years later, it was introduced – in spite of the misgivings of India's national government.

Landlords were restricted to holding about 22 acres (excluding orchards and forest) and – after much consideration – they were not awarded compensation. Tens of thousands of small-scale peasant farmers gained land, in a social revolution as bold as any that India has seen. Land reform in Kashmir was, according to a historian of agrarian reform, 'more progressive than in the rest of India' and 'proceeded more democratically than in the rest of the country' (Iqbal, 2018; Kotovsky, 1964: 114–115). There were loopholes which some landowners exploited to limit the impact of the measures, and corruption and nepotism in its implementation also blunted the impact. The reforms did not end the leasing of land and landless labourers benefitted much less than small tenant farmers from the curtailing of the large landed estates. The preponderance of Hindus among the landlords gave rise to charges that land reform was a communal measure aimed at benefitting the state's Muslim majority. Nevertheless, for all the faults, Sheikh Abdullah's determination to achieve a fairer distribution of land changed the face of rural Jammu and Kashmir.

There was a further aspect of *New Kashmir* which is both surprising and significant – its approach to gender. Clause twelve of the proposed constitution declared:

> Women citizens shall be accorded equal rights with men in all fields of national life: economic, cultural, political, and in the state services. These rights shall be realised by affording women the right to work in every employment upon equal terms and for equal wages with men. Women shall be ensured rest, social insurance and education equally with men. The law shall give special protection to the interests of mother and child. The provision of pregnancy leave with pay and the establishment of a wide network of maternity homes, nurseries and kindergartens shall further secure these rights.

This followed closely the wording of article 122 in the Stalin constitution and could be regarded as a reflex copying of the model on which *New Kashmir* was based. Yet the document also included a four-page women's charter, which was a substantial statement of women's political, economic, social, legal, educational and cultural rights. This had a resoundingly progressive tone extending to a commitment to the right to consent to marriage and to divorce, the right to 'enter any profession or trade or do any kind of work of which she considers she is capable', and the establishment of separate colleges for women alongside women's access to men's colleges. Some within the National Conference believed that Freda Bedi helped to ensure this commitment to gender issues – and while she, in contrast to her husband, never sought to claim any responsibility for the manifesto, it is difficult to imagine that her role was (as Sheikh Abdullah suggested) restricted to that of typist.

There were other indications of the National Conference's wish to win support from women. The cover of the English edition of *New Kashmir* depicted a flag-waving woman, rather crudely drawn, but politically assertive rather than decorative. Her flag was that of the National Conference, a hand plough in white on a red background – an emblem which, as the visiting British Communist Rajani

Palme Dutt remarked, bore more than a passing similarity to the Soviet hammer and sickle (Dutt, 1946: 319–326). The woman is believed to have been a representation of Zuni Gujjari, a renowned National Conference activist from an underprivileged background. When in the aftermath of the repulse of the invading tribesmen, Sheikh Abdullah's supporters published a conspicuously well-produced propaganda tract entitled *Kashmir Defends Democracy*, Zuni Gujjari was again depicted on the cover. She was shown in a striking red silhouette, lying on the ground and aiming a rifle – the work of the noted artist Sobha Singh. This was set against the background of a photograph of Kashmir's Women's Self Defence Corps walking with rifles on their shoulders. This women's militia along with the much larger men's contingent, another largely Communist initiative, was set up when Srinagar was in danger of being overrun, and was another startling indication of the increased role for women at this time of transition and political mobilisation. Several of the women who joined the militia were involved in one of the more tangible expressions of *New Kashmir* – the setting up of a Government College for Women in a building which once housed the widows of the princely family – though the proto-feminism evident in the manifesto did not reflect, or lead to the creation of, an enduring grassroots women's movement (Kanjwal, 2018).

The *New Kashmir* manifesto was handed over in person to the maharaja in July 1944. It was formally adopted by the National Conference at its annual congress held in Srinagar in September. There were some muted misgivings about the determinedly left-wing tone of the document, as well as unhappiness about the continued tolerance of princely rule, but little sustained opposition (Jan, 2006: 80–83; Saraf, 1977: 643–646). One of the most prominent Kashmiri Communists noted a sharp discrepancy between the militancy of the manifesto and the outlook of National Conference activists. 'There was an air of unreality about the whole operation', N.N. Raina recalled.

> One thing that is difficult to understand is that the programme was not produced in a high tide of mass upsurge ... The lack of resistance to its adoption at that time can be attributed to the apathy and scepticism of the cadres rather than the high tide of militancy in the state.
>
> (Raina, 1980: 121)

But in what perhaps might be a self-serving argument, Raina asserted that the detailed socialist blueprint of *New Kashmir* contributed to Kashmiris' 'political enlightenment'.

It is not clear whether Freda and B.P.L. Bedi attended the 1944 annual session of the National Conference, but they were certainly present the following year. A remarkable photo taken during the 1945 gathering includes the Bedis, two future prime ministers of Kashmir and three future prime ministers of India. Jawaharlal Nehru had just been released from jail and promptly travelled to Kashmir to join his daughter, Indira Gandhi. Among the other guests at the session were a Pathan leader from Baluchistan, Abdul Samad Khan Achakzai, and the

The making of the New Kashmir *manifesto* 27

Pathan nationalist Khan Abdul Ghaffar Khan, sometimes known as 'the Frontier Gandhi'. In the photograph, Khan is carrying a baby, almost certainly Indira's son, Rajiv. Standing behind this illustrious row of political leaders are Sheikh Abdullah and his colleague and later rival Bakshi Ghulam Mohammad. On the right of the group is Freda Bedi (she is clearly pregnant – her son, Kabir, was born in Lahore in January 1946) and behind her, slightly hidden from the camera, is B.P.L. Bedi. Freda and her baby son were in Kashmir the following year when the eruption of the Quit Kashmir movement and the detention of Sheikh Abdullah threw the Kashmir Valley into ferment. The state authorities issued an 'externment' or deportation order against her, which she ignored. She at one point famously dressed in a burka-style garment to meet National Conference leaders operating underground in Srinagar. When Rajani Palme Dutt – on a long visit to India – went to Srinagar as a show of support for Sheikh Abdullah, he was briefed beforehand in Lahore by B.P.L. Bedi and contacted Freda Bedi once in Srinagar.

The violence surrounding Partition forced the Bedi family out of Lahore. They made Kashmir their new home, arriving in Srinagar in an Indian military plane in December 1947. Freda enrolled in the women's militia, worked with refugees and became a lecturer at the Government College for Women, as well as looking after her family. She was entirely invested in the New Kashmir project. 'Kashmir with its Socialist Government [and] its young leaders can lead India, rebuild this miserable Country', she wrote in a letter to an old friend. 'I've great faith in it, [and] love for it, too. It is beautiful, rich in talent [and] natural resources' (Bedi, 1949). B.P.L. became a key figure in the administration, though with imprecise responsibilities: advising on policy, writing speeches and drafting communications with Delhi, seeking to establish new commercial links to replace those disrupted by Partition and heading a counter-propaganda operation to challenge a barrage of criticism from Pakistan and its supporters. Bedi was proud of the network of informers he created in Srinagar and insisted that their purpose was simply to allow rapid rebuttal of misinformation and market rumours – but it clearly had the potential to be used for a more sinister purpose. Sheikh Abdullah was more effective as a mobiliser than as an administrator and he wasn't instinctively a pluralist. His intolerance of opposition, which extended to the jailing of some of his former allies, took the shine off the idealism of *New Kashmir*. He formally became the prime minister of Jammu and Kashmir in March 1948, an appointment which reflected the political eclipse of the Dogra dynasty. He faced no challenge at the ballot box. India's Constituent Assembly began its deliberations several months before independence, and the constitution drafted principally by B.R. Ambedkar came into force in January 1950. Jammu and Kashmir's four representatives took their seats in the Constituent Assembly only in June 1949 – and unlike in other princely states, none of these representatives was elected. Sheikh Abdullah was given authority, in the light of the disturbed conditions after the first India-Pakistan war, to nominate the state's representatives. India's constitution included a clause which continues to excite political controversy, even though its practical importance has been greatly diluted over the decades. Article 370 gives Jammu and Kashmir special status within the Indian Union, reflecting both the state's disputed accession and (*sotto voce*) its unique status as a Muslim majority area bordering Pakistan. Jammu and Kashmir was to have its own laws, flag, definition of citizenship – and constitution.

That is how, almost two years after India's constitution came into force, Sheikh Abdullah delivered his opening address to Jammu and Kashmir's Constituent Assembly – an elected body, though the National Conference won all the seats, all but three without a contest. 'Today is our day of destiny', he declared. 'We meet here today, in this palace hall, once the symbol of unquestioned monarchical authority, as free citizens of the New Kashmir for which we have so long struggled' (Jammu and Kashmir Constituent Assembly, 1951). This referencing of *New Kashmir* was a repeated theme of Sheikh Abdullah's initial period in power. It has been suggested that the document served both as 'a developmental roadmap' and, in the absence of any other statement of democratic principles and developmental goals, as 'the de facto constitution' (Iqbal, 2018). It was another five years before the state's constitution was adopted, confirming that Jammu and Kashmir was 'an integral part' of India; by then, Sheikh Abdullah was in detention. The imprint of *New Kashmir* survived in a statement that the 'prime object of the State consistent with the ideals and objectives of the freedom movement in "New Kashmir" shall be the promotion of the welfare of the mass of the people by establishing and preserving a socialist order of society'. But beyond an imprecise commitment to a planned economy, there was little detail offered to flesh out what a socialist order of society entailed. The gender provisions of *New Kashmir* were one of the few aspects to appear in broadly similar terms in the state's 1956 constitution. This asserted women's right to equal pay for equal work as well as the right to maternity benefits, to 'reasonable maintenance' for those divorced or abandoned by their husbands and 'the right to full equality in all social, education, political and legal matters'.

By the time that Nehru took to writing to Sheikh Abdullah warning about B.P.L. Bedi, the subject of his censure had already become keenly aware of Delhi's disapproval. Bedi recalled in later years that:

> one of the big jobs about which I feel really happy, was helping in the expropriation of landlords without compensation, and cancellation of indebtedness too. So, the Kashmir policy was very, very soulful in this sense, but at that time it was not without its pains, because very great pressure was exerted by the Government of India for my being sent away from Kashmir, because they felt that leftist policies would be going on more and more adamantly ... if I stayed on there.
>
> (Bedi, 1969)

Certainly Josef Korbel – a Czechoslovak diplomat who was appointed to the United Nations Commission on India and Pakistan and was later granted asylum in the United States – regarded Bedi as the Communist *eminence grise* behind Sheikh Abdullah's government. 'If one compares the program and policy of the Communist satellites in Europe with New Kashmir and the practices of the

Kashmiri government', Korbel complained, 'one cannot escape the conclusion that Kashmir has already reached the first step towards communisation' (Korbel, 1966: 198, 254, 218).

There was an injustice behind some of the sharp criticisms of Bedi. His primary loyalty was to Sheikh Abdullah, not the CPI. The Communists in Kashmir were in any case sharply divided, and their political influence was curtailed by Sheikh Abdullah's decisive action against left-wingers running the militia. The continuing Communist influence in Jammu and Kashmir was above all through a very small number of influential fellow travellers, who were sympathetic to the CPI – and the Soviet Union – but not party members. Of these the most prominent was G.M. Sadiq, who was Jammu and Kashmir's prime minister (and then chief minister when the post was redesignated) for seven years in the latter part of the 1960s. Bedi himself appears to have been moved out of the most sensitive aspects of government and given a role in education. He worked along with his wife in revising school textbooks – an important task, but not central to the work of the state government.

To add to Bedi's distress, the Communist Party of India – which adopted a sharp change of line shortly after independence and put much of its effort behind a peasant uprising in Telangana in southern India – was critical of Bedi's role in achieving land redistribution by legislative measures:

> Now this was the one act which earned me the severest condemnation from the Communist Party, as to why all these measures were not brought about in the Telangana manner: that is by murder of officials, murder of landlords, and then taking over lands and all that. To that I said, "I have never come across a more stupid approach than this. When the entire national movement was adopting the programme, which I myself had drafted, and then the entire national movement plus the government ... without a single mishap the whole thing was implemented. You don't realise that in Kashmir it was not just a mere handing over of power to the national movement ... It was virtually, if you look at it realistically, a seizure of power."
>
> (Bedi, 1969)

Bedi recalled with an abiding sense of anger that he was forced out of the CPI. 'I knew that my expulsion from the party was more a reflection on the party itself than upon myself. So I said, "Don't bother. Leave it."' Sheikh Abdullah, on the other hand – in his idiosyncratic 'as told to' reminiscences – put a very different complexion on the political meaning of the land reform measures, suggesting that it was not an indication of Communist influence but a means of blocking such influence. He asserted that he

> purged our region of germs of Communism by implementing the land reforms and waiving off the farmers' agricultural loans. By these measures we had, if you like, pulled off the carpet from beneath the feet of the Communists in the state.
>
> (Abdullah, 2013: 413)

It was a curious repudiation of those Abdullah had himself summoned to help assemble his political arsenal.

By his own account, B.P.L. Bedi decided after the convening of Jammu and Kashmir's Constituent Assembly that his work was done. 'So there was really no political job for me and I had started to search my heart, whether now for the sake of the apples and pears of Kashmir it was justified for me to stay' (Bedi, 1969). This was only part of the story. His family recall a breach with Sheikh Abdullah, which they believe – though this may be an unreliable memory – was because Bedi advised against Sheikh Abdullah's questioning of the finality of the state's accession to India. By the spring of 1953, Bedi had moved to Delhi. His years working with Sheikh Abdullah in Srinagar were the only period in his life when he had regular employment and income. Freda Bedi had to find an income to replace that of her husband, and she took a short assignment with the United Nations in Burma (now Myanmar). While there, she met prominent Buddhist monks and had a moment of enlightenment (her family describe it more as a moment of crisis) which drew her towards Buddhism. Shortly after her return to India, she took personal vows which, it seems, included celibacy and in subsequent years she became a Tibetan Buddhist nun. For a while once settled in Delhi, B.P.L. Bedi was a member of a pressure group supportive of Sheikh Abdullah, the Friends of New Kashmir Committee established by Mridula Sarabhai, but this was about his last entanglement with politics. Faced with the loss of his job and political role and the fracturing of his marriage, B.P.L. too went through a breakdown of sorts. He embraced the occult and other forms of mysticism and spirituality. He never renounced Communism but nor did he actively advocate for it any more.

Bakshi Ghulam Mohammad, when he replaced Sheikh Abdullah as the prime minister of Jammu and Kashmir in August 1953, continued to talk of the goal of New Kashmir. Although he was an opponent of the left, he shared many of the progressive ideals which underpinned the National Conference (Kanjwal, 2017). The term 'New Kashmir' was also used at times as an invocation or badge, an assertion that while Sheikh Abdullah had gone, his political legacy was not being repudiated. From the moment of Abdullah's overthrow and arrest, the most burning aspect of Kashmir's political life became managing the unequal relationship with the Indian government. On that, *New Kashmir* offered little in the way of a compass bearing. A manifesto is always very much of its moment, serving an immediate political purpose. *New Kashmir* confirmed the radicalism, ambition and intellectual dynamism of the National Conference and helped to bolster its hegemony in the popular politics of the Kashmir Valley. The way in which *New Kashmir* was compiled reveals Sheikh Abdullah's political pragmatism. The manner by which Communists assembled *New Kashmir* doesn't diminish the importance of the document, but it does enrich an understanding of Sheikh Abdullah's brand of nationalism during the brief period when it was the dominant political force in the Kashmir Valley (Whitehead, 2018).

Seventy-five years on from its drafting, *New Kashmir* is remembered but not read. It is a testament to the manifesto's originality and the manner in which it defined what was then the main trend within Kashmiri nationalism that its reputation has lasted for so long. That is rare among what are so often ephemeral documents. *New Kashmir*'s near contemporary – *Let Us Face the Future*, the reforming manifesto on which the British Labour Party won the 1945 general election – is similarly venerated because of the political moment it captured. Yet one manifesto led, in a roundabout way, to the pulling of the political carpet from underneath the other. The Labour Party document committed Britain's new government to 'the advancement of India to responsible self-government'. The manner in which that was executed, and the failure to establish the enduring status of Jammu and Kashmir before Britain's withdrawal, sparked the conflict about who governs Kashmir. Kashmiri politics and public life have become so wrapped up in the issue of status – whether Kashmir is an integral part of India, or should have an exceptional level of autonomy within India – that a manifesto which is silent on this issue seems obsolete. There appears to be little space these days for a progressive nationalism in Kashmir.

Works cited

Abdullah, Sheikh Mohammad (2013). *The Blazing Chinar: An Autobiography*. Srinagar: Gulshan.
Bedi, B.P.L. (1969). Oral History Interview. Nehru Memorial Museum and Library, New Delhi.
Bedi, B.P.L., and Freda Bedi (eds.) (1933–34). *India Analysed*, 3 Vols. London: Victor Gollancz.
Bedi, Freda (1949). Letter to Oliver Chandler. 19 January. Letter in the possession of the Bedi family.
Bose, Sumantra (2009). *Kashmir: Roots of Conflict, Paths to Peace*. Cambridge, MA: Harvard University Press.
Dhar, D.N. (2004). *Kashmir: The Land and Its Management from Ancient to Modern Times*. New Delhi: Kanishka.
Dutt, Rajani Palme (1946). 'Travel Notes No. 5'. *Labour Monthly* 28(10), 319–326.
Gangulee, N. (ed.) (1943). *Russia Horizon: An Anthology*. London: George Allen & Unwin.
Giyas-ud-Din, Peer (1999). *Jammu and Kashmir State and Society: Communist Movement in Kashmir*. Jammu: Jay Kay Book House.
Iqbal, Sehar (2018). *Social Impact on State Development Policy in Jammu and Kashmir: 1948 to 1988*. PhD thesis, University of Kashmir.
Jammu and Kashmir Constituent Assembly (1951). 'Opening Address by the Hon'ble Sheikh Mohammed Abdullah, Srinagar, November 5, 1951'. Srinagar: Constituent Assembly Secretariat.
Jan, Asifa (2006). *Naya Kashmir: An Appraisal*. Srinigar: Zeba Publications.
Kanjwal, Hafsa (2017). *Building a New Kashmir: Bakshi Ghulam Mohammad and the Politics of State-Formation in a Disputed Territory (1953–1963)*. PhD thesis, University of Michigan.
Kanjwal, Hafsa (2018). 'The New Kashmiri Woman: State-Led Feminism in *Naya Kashmir*'. *Economic & Political Weekly*, 53(47). 1 December [online]. Available at www.epw.in/journal/2018/47/review-womens-studies/new-kashmiri-woman.html [accessed 15 February 2019].
Kanth, Idrees (2018). *Seeking Futures, Shaping Pasts: The Ambiguities that Have Defined the Political Discourse of Aazadi in Kashmir*. PhD thesis, University of Leiden.
Korbel, Josef (1966). *Danger in Kashmir*. Princeton, NJ: Princeton University Press.

Kotovsky, Grigory (1964). *Agrarian Reforms in India*. New Delhi: People's Publishing House, 114–115.

Nehru, Jawaharalal (1978). *Selected Works of Jawarharlal Nehru*, 2nd series, Vol. 11, edited by S. Gopal. New Delhi: B.R. Publishing.

New Kashmir (n.d.). *New Kashmir Manifesto* (1944). Kashmir Bureau of Information, New Delhi.

Rai, Mridu (2018). 'The Indian Constituent Assembly and the Making of Hindus and Muslims in Jammu and Kashmir'. *Asian Affairs* 49(2), 201–221.

Raina, N.N. (1980). *Kashmir Politics and Imperialist Manoeuvres, 1846–1980*. New Delhi: Patriot.

Saraf, Muhammad Yusuf (1977 and 1979). *Kashmiris Fight for Freedom*, 2 Vols. Lahore: Ferozsons.

Surjeet, Harkishan Singh (1995). *A History of the Kisan Sabha*. Calcutta: National Book Agency.

Taseer, Christabel Bilqees (1986). *The Kashmir of Sheikh Muhammad Abdullah*. Lahore: Ferozsons.

The Soviet Socialist Constitution (1937). London: Russia Today Society.

Whitehead, Andrew (2007a). *A Mission in Kashmir*. New Delhi: Viking Penguin.

Whitehead, Andrew (2007b). Interview with Pran Nath Jalali, New Delhi. March.

Whitehead, Andrew (2007c). Interview with Pran Chopra, New Delhi. April.

Whitehead, Andrew (2010). 'The People's Militia: Communists and Kashmiri Nationalism in the 1940s'. *Twentieth Century Communism: A Journal of International History* (2), 141–168.

Whitehead, Andrew (2018). 'The Rise and Fall of New Kashmir'. In: Chitralekha Zutshi (ed.) *Kashmir: History, Politics, Representation*. Cambridge: Cambridge University Press, pp. 70–88.

Whitehead, Andrew (2019). *The Lives of Freda: The Political, Spiritual and Personal Journeys of Freda Bedi*. Delhi: Speaking Tiger.

Zutshi, Chitralekha (2003). *Languages of Belonging: Islam, Regional Identity, and the Making of Kashmir*. Delhi: Permanent Black.

2 Half-widows and the travesty of justice in Indian-administered Kashmir

Sohini Chatterjee

'I searched [for] him for months. Except for the army camps I searched for him everywhere. And one day I just gave up', Fatima reveals, emphasising 'we are illiterate people. In this far-away unreported world we do not have any information how to proceed with the case legally' (Umar, 2013). Fatima's personhood in conflict-torn, violence-ravaged Kashmir is constructed externally where she is identified as a 'half-widow': an identity label that reveals structural violence, dispossession, the scourge of militarisation, precarity and helplessness. Fatima has no access to information on her husband; no recourse to any justice system that is able to furnish this information to her. Fatima is one among thousands of 'half-widows' who are the indirect victims of the crime of enforced disappearance whose direct victims were their now missing husbands. According to the Association of the Parents of Disappeared Persons (APDP), since 1989 approximately 8,000 to 10,000 men have disappeared, or have been made to disappear from Kashmir, resulting in close to 1,500 'half-widows' (Parthasarathy, 2016); other sources claim the number is as high as 2,500 (Bashir, 2011). Half-widows in Kashmir are essentially women waiting for news of their husbands, living in the hope that they might return to their families one day, all the while struggling to make ends meet owing to the political economy of gendered labour in a male-dominated, militarised, conflict-ridden region where women's mobility is limited and obstructed by patriarchy and the conflict situation that sustains it. Paul D'Souza writes that

> after the disappearance of their husband, women are placed on the threshold between waiting and living; of knowing and not knowing what comes next. They occupy a liminal space that denies them both the status of a wife and the dignity of a widow.
>
> (D'Souza, 2016, 28)

And yet, they have to carry the burdens of a widow which crucially entails the struggle of providing for their children alone and a socio-cultural impediment to remarriage.

On December 26, 2013, it was decreed by some religious clerics that half-widows in Kashmir could remarry four years after their husband's disappearance.

It was a decree that came 22 years after the first disappearance and 7 years since the last (*Business Standard*, 2015). Many of the half-widows in Kashmir had by that time spent a considerable part of their lives battling gendered precarity where remarriage was religiously and socio-culturally disapproved of and hence not a viable option for women, especially those with children. Remarriage in Kashmir, even after the decree, is often impractical for most of the half-widows for whom the decree has come two decades too late. Injustice has taken and continues to take many forms in Kashmir. Half-widows are particularly hard hit and constitute one of the most economically marginalised sections of women in Kashmir who, in the absence of their husband, are economically reliant on their marital and natal families for survival along with their children. Ration cards, a source of economic relief, are difficult to obtain as is the transfer of their husband's property and bank accounts in the absence of a death certificate. As reported by *Business Standard*, 'under Islamic jurisprudence, a widow with children gets one-eighth of her husband's property. A widow without children gets one-fourth. A half-widow, till her husband is declared dead, gets nothing' (*Business Standard*, 2015). Violence survived and suffered by half-widows occurs along the lines of multiple absences: of their husband, information, rights and justice.

Taking gendered vulnerabilities into account Kashmir is seen to illustrate, in no uncertain terms, how insecurities are often shaped by inter-state relations while also demonstrating how state violence intensifies precarity, violence and gendered insecurities in conflict zones. Unheard margins in the world's underdeveloped and developing states have been long ignored within the discipline of International Relations (IR), as has gendered violence in those regions and spaces. The first edition of Cynthia Enloe's *Bananas, Beaches, and Bases: Making Feminist Sense of International Politics* asks a fundamentally inconvenient question to the discipline – 'where are the women?' – exposing masculine universalist claims through which IR had evolved. Identifying that 'there is a serious flaw in the analytical economy and in the research strategy that flows from it', Enloe (1996) asserts that the discipline presumes that 'margins, silences and bottom rungs are so naturally marginal, silent and far from power' that the structures and processes through which they have come to occupy its marginal locality do not merit investigation by rationalist investigators (188). Enloe further argues that

> a consequence of this presumption is that the actual amount and amazing variety of power that are required to keep the voices on the margins from having the right language and enough volume to be heard at the centre in ways that might send shivers up and down the ladder are never fully tallied.
> (1996, 188)

However, in IR, as in other disciplines, feminism has not been inclusive of variously marginalised women in underdeveloped and developing countries. Chandra Talpade Mohanty, Ann Russo and Lourdes Torres (1991) argue that Western radical and liberal feminist scholarship have addressed women as a homogeneous category, in disregard of Third World women, thereby appropriating 'the pluralities of simultaneous location of different groups of women in social class and ethnic frameworks', dissociating them from 'historical and political agency' (71–72). Western feminism's 'ethnocentric universalism' (Mohanty, 1991, 55) views women as collectively powerless, oppressed and subjugated without accounting for 'the material and ideological specificities' that render particular groups of women powerless owing to skewed structural dynamics in their specific locational contexts (Mohanty, 1991, 56–57).

However, recognition of this diversity and the critical attention it merits could not be extended by Western feminism due to its own imperial universalism. A call to bridge this gap in knowledge production was urged by postcolonial feminist theorists who realised that feminist IR research needed to make space for gender-based postcolonial interventions to expand its horizons. What needed to be examined was how formal equality does not preclude the denial of equal rights and access to political and economic power in developing states and societies. Investigation was necessary to problematise functions of postcolonial states and their often imperial behaviour leading to the creation of gendered margins where women are overwhelmingly disempowered (Parashar et al., 2018, 6). Within postcolonial states, marginalisation of some regions and gendered experiences are far more acute than those of others owing to the challenges of nation-building efforts in the postcolonial world and how those were mitigated by postcolonial states, often acting in imperial ways, creating peripheries that have been systemically rendered vulnerable to violence and injustice. Kashmir has emerged as one such peripheral borderland in India where conflict has created gendered insecurities owing to the politics of national security and volatile inter-state ties between India and Pakistan. The injustices suffered by half-widows have to be contextualised through a reading of the political history of the region.

Historical background

Kashmir, the 'unfinished business of partition between India and Pakistan' is a veritable inferno and has been so since at least 1989. That year an insurgency began after prolonged 'locally motivated, non-violent struggles for popular sovereignty and political self-determination' were brought to near exhaustion, without producing the intended effect (Chatterjee, 2011, 58). Promises of history are often undermined by political expediency. Kashmir, destabilised by decades of political mayhem and carnage, attests to this. In October 1947, Muslim-majority Kashmir – more prominently contiguous to Western Punjab and North-West Frontier Province (NWFP) than eastern Punjab in India – was made to accede to the Indian Union when Pashtun tribesmen from NWFP's Hazara district launched an offensive into Jammu and Kashmir. The state's Hindu Dogra autocrat Hari Singh, finding himself ill-equipped to tackle this challenge militarily, sought New Delhi's assistance, which ultimately led him to sign an Instrument of Accession to India (Bose, 2009, 36). In November 1947, however, Jawaharlal Nehru, India's prime minister, acknowledged the contentious nature of Kashmir's accession and promised that a plebiscite would be held in due course, with the assistance of the United Nations and under the watchful eye of the international community, to determine Kashmir's fate. This was the first of many elusive political promises that would mire the Valley in enduring unrest producing tragic consequences deeply gendered in nature.

In 1987, when moves were made to constitute a legislative assembly in Jammu and Kashmir through proper electoral procedures, such efforts were actively undermined. The Jammu and Kashmir (J&K) National Conference is the descendant of J&K's first political party founded in 1932 by Sheikh Abdullah and Chaudhry Ghulam Abbas, the All Jammu and Kashmir Muslim Conference. Once Abbas loyalists split from the party, the NC came to be identified with Sheikh Abdullah and was guided by this vision and was a significant mobiliser of Kashmiris. However, two decades after Abdullah's death, 'far removed from its popular base and very much the tool of the vested interests of a narrow political elite', it joined forces with the Indian National Conference (Bose, 2009, 47–48). In 1987, in violation of the integrity of Indian democracy, the failing National Conference, in concert with the Indian National Congress, declared its own candidate the winner over the leader of the hugely popular coalition of anti-establishment parties constituting the Muslim United Front (MUF). As protests broke out against vote-rigging and other kinds of electoral fraud, the MUF candidate, its supporters and electoral manager were all hauled up and imprisoned without an arrest warrant and were later denied fair trials (Bose, 2009, 49). Bukhari argues that before armed militancy began in 1989, electoral malfeasance in Kashmir destabilised democracy.

As promises of a plebiscite increasingly started to ring hollow, democratic spaces started to shrink and registering pacific dissent proved to be inadequate. Young men took up arms against the Indian state that they felt had systematically denied them the right to self-determination. Olapally (2008) observes that, 'in Kashmir, separatist tendencies were least when democracy and autonomy were strongest' (116). The insurgency coincided with the collapse of democracy and ushered in an era of militarisation which then further countermanded democracy having dire consequences for human rights in the region. Kashmiris were denied voting rights in what were highly unreliable elections even as 'mainland' India, barring some cases of electoral notoriety, was able to vote in free and fair elections upholding India's international status as the world's largest democracy. Moreover, as educational facilities improved and mass media became more accessible to Kashmiris, awareness of their marginalisation led to growing resentment against the Indian state (Ganguly, 1996, 83). Ganguly (1996) further argues that in a polyethnic society, minorities gradually gain awareness of political and economic discrimination against them. Should this awareness be gained at a time when institutional mechanisms to express dissent are absent or are malfunctioning, dissent against the state turns to violence, demonstrating an intention and effort to subvert the status quo. The state, in such trying times, either makes concessions taking cognisance of grievances or utilises tools of repression to muzzle dissenting voices (93). In the case of Kashmir, India did the latter.

India's recourse to repression was partly an effort to maintain its national unity owing to the fact that it considers Kashmir 'integral' to its nationhood. But it was largely compounded by Pakistan's role in the insurgency. Benazir Bhutto provided political support to Kashmiri insurgents and Pakistan's Directorate of Inter-Service Intelligence, or the ISI as it is popularly known, provided insurgents with materials and adequate support 'funneling aid across the ceasefire Line of Control leading from Pakistan-controlled Azad Kashmir/Baltistan into the Indian controlled valley of Kashmir' (Scott, 2011, 63). The ISI, as an intelligence agency, is Pakistan's first line of defence, providing its government information on probable national security threats. ISI's organisational structure is monolithic and it is vested with the task of supervising both external and internal intelligence operations in the state. Until the 1970s, the ISI's external intelligence agenda largely revolved around India (Chengappa, 2000, 1857). Constituted within the Pakistani Army to fulfil the need for inter-service intelligence cooperation, its primary task includes: protecting Pakistan's interests, to keep political opposition in check and to sustain and secure military rule in Pakistan (Gregory, 2007, 1014). Winchell (2003) argues that the ISI serves as a 'principal liaison' with militant Islamic organisations, many of which have now been declared terrorist organisations. Joint Intelligence North is a vital part of ISI that has provided 'financial aid, military assistance, and logistical assistance to militants in the region' (379). He further points out that Islamic militants in the region are provided by the ISI with 'indoctrination programs and runs training camps, which in turn produce seasoned and motivated Islamic militants experienced in the use of advanced weapons systems and explosives' (380).

Pakistan also sponsored various Islamic militant groups from Afghanistan and Pakistan to fight the Indian military in Kashmir. Behera argues that the insurgency started off as an 'indigenous underground' mobilisation of people who associated themselves with the Jammu and Kashmir Liberation Front (JKLF). This subsequently turned into a mass movement calling for *azaadi* (freedom), unprecedented in its intensity. In the next phase, the insurgency developed and then diverged, clamouring for two different ends: one pressed for secession and the other seemed to be in favour of accession to Pakistan. It was later guided by a smaller group of militants who were well armed and well trained but did not belong in Kashmir (Behera, 2006, 145).

The Indian state – threatened, affronted and riled up by the 'proxy war' staged by a Pakistan that coveted Kashmir and wanted to keep India perpetually off balance – employed brute force to suppress the insurgency, provoking a never-ending spiral of insurgency and counter-insurgency that claimed lives and inflicted insurmountable suffering on the living. No distinction was made between those indigenous militants who wanted the state to recognise their right to self-determination and those 'foreign militants' whose stakes in the conflict were clearly different. Bose argues that the Indian government seemed unable to distinguish between pro-Pakistani groups and those who were asserting their right to self-determination. This led them to homogenise all insurgents as 'pro-Pakistan', serving the purpose of inspiring 'para-military and army *jawans* with the belief that they are fighting Pakistan on the soil of Kashmir' (Bose, Mohan, Navlakha and Banerjee, 1990, 657).

In turn, 'the internal processes that caused the rebellion' were relegated to the background and 'externalising internal conflicts' helped 'anaesthetise' the people from protesting against curtailment of their freedoms (Navlakha, 2002, 3423). The infamous and dreaded Armed Forces (Special Powers) Act or the AFSPA was instituted with absolute powers vested in it, enabling security forces to discipline and regulate 'disturbed' areas on their own terms without the fear of retributive justice. AFSPA allows security forces to shoot and kill according to their whims and fancies, arrest without warrant, search private and public spaces alike, and destroy shelters on the basis of mere suspicion.

> AFSPA violates the nonderogable provisions of international human rights law, including the right to life and the right to be free from arbitrary deprivation of liberty, torture, and cruel, inhuman, or degrading punishment, as enshrined in the International Covenant on Civil and Political Rights (ICCPR), to which India is a signatory. The AFSPA also violates article 21 of the constitution of India. Repressive legislation such as the AFSPA allows military forces to wage war against recalcitrant populations with impunity.
> (Kazi, 2015, 680)

Despite the evident dangers and history of excess in the Valley owing to an AFSPA-sponsored culture of impunity, the Indian state continues to validate it for security in Kashmir. Hence, the trials and tribulations that are now intimately enmeshed in the lived realities of hundreds of half-widows in Kashmir are entrenched in the failure of democracy. The preponderance of the logic of national security and heavy-handedness of security forces normalised by militarism and impunity in the Valley create conditions of unliveability sustained by the problem of unknowability. In this highly volatile context where politics is abandoned in favour of national security considerations, justice for half-widows provokes and entails questions carrying significant political weight.

The problem and politics of unknowability

In 2011, the Jammu and Kashmir State Human Rights Commission (SHRC) conducted a probe into the unmarked graves that are scattered across Jammu and Kashmir, finding evidence of 2,156 unidentified bodies across 38 sites in 3 districts of north Kashmir, namely Baramulla, Bandipore and Kupwara. The Special Investigating Team's report suggested that there is 'every possibility' that some of those unidentified bodies could be of victims of enforced disappearances (*The Hindu*, 2011). Many of the victims' families also expressed apprehensions that their relatives could be buried somewhere in those unmarked graves (Ashiq, 2012). Soudiya Qutab in her work presents one of the tragic narratives of a half-widow who would visit various places with her son – despite awareness of the risks involved – hoping to find clues about her missing husband. A shovel in hand, she would often resort to digging graves in search of closure (Qutab, 2012, 271), asserting her right to a history that was denied to her and her child. Either censure, or erasure, of individual histories accompanies the crime of enforced disappearance; however, the right of victim families to the knowledge of these histories holds critical significance for questions of justice as well as closure. But efforts to uncover them come with difficult challenges of a varying nature.

In 2012, the Association of Parents of Disappeared Persons (APDP) submitted 507 documented cases of enforced disappearances from villages in the districts of Baramulla and Bandipore in north Kashmir, urging the state government to undertake DNA testing and other forensic methods to identify the bodies. This petition was filed a day after the government had claimed that India did not have the financial ability to carry out elaborate DNA investigations into unmarked graves; even if it attempted such sampling it could take many years (*The Indian Express*, 2012). Despite being ardently pushed for by activists, DNA investigations have not begun as of now. The problem of unknowability, however, only has its beginning in such official laxity regarding DNA testing. This is not the only way in which information is withheld from half-widows and victims' families which contributes to the endurance of the problem of unknowability.

There have also been cases where men were picked up in crackdowns but the army simply denied having taken them into custody when faced with anxious questioning from wives of the disappeared men (Qutab, 2012, 260). The police have on many occasions refused to register a First Information Report (FIR) claiming that the person in question was a militant and had crossed the Line of Control (Qutab, 2012, 261; Bhattacharya, 2016, 30; APDP, 2011). Since DNA tests have not been conducted, there is no conclusive proof of death, and with the refusal of the police to file a FIR, it becomes difficult to establish that these disappearances have been enforced. Hence, unknowability pertaining to the disappearances is a problem which is deeply political in nature, having been actively backed by state forces over several decades. The impossibility of ascertaining the 'truth' leads to the active de-politicisation of this issue, which is a choice that political leaders have made over many years. A report released by APDP in 2011, titled 'Half Widow, Half Wife?', presents a narrative of a woman who was identified as a 'half-widow' for two months until the discovery of her husband's grave. The body was exhumed but she was not handed over his remains as the 'police insisted that the army would never allow that' (APDP, 2011, 8).

Thus, evidently the state has successfully orchestrated a disabling quagmire from where justice seems improbable, as the very basis on which it can be pursued is frequently rendered suspect. Political and governing authorities dispute motivations for justice of victims' families in various ways through many convoluted propositions. Seema Kazi, writing on sexual violence and the culture of impunity in Kashmir that precludes the possibility of justice, observes, 'the impunity of action that security forces enjoy in Kashmir subverted the normal law enforcement machinery centred on the police, destroyed the professional integrity and autonomy of the local police, and converted it into an appendage of security forces' (Kazi, 2014, 31).

The APDP claims that a. majority of those who became victims of enforced disappearances have been killed by security forces. Refuting it, the government's opposing claim is that men who are 'missing' crossed the Line of Control to join militant groups in Pakistan. In 2003, Mufti Mohammed Sayeed, who was then the leader of the opposition in the state, had said that many of those 'reported missing' since 1990 were actually in Pakistan where they had gone to receive training in militancy and never came back (Human Rights Watch, 2011). In a similar vein in 2011, then Chief Minister of Jammu and Kashmir Omar Abdullah declared that every individual who 'disappeared' was not killed. Some are now living in Pakistan and Pakistan-occupied Kashmir (PoK) as drivers, shopkeepers and labourers. Some of them have married and have children (Bukhari, 2011). The political elite in the region, despite their divergent locations on the political spectrum, likes to privilege this narrative in opposition to alternative possibilities suggested by human rights groups, activists and victims' families in the Valley that hold the state responsible for refusing accountability in cases of disappearance.

This goes to show that not only has the government not been particularly keen on conducting DNA tests on unidentified bodies and has been reluctant to carry out investigations into cases of enforced disappearances, it has also tried to delegitimise fears of half-widows that their husbands might have been tortured and killed by security forces. Instead, governing authorities have insisted time and again that those who disappeared often did so out of their own volition and could be leading altogether different lives in Pakistan. Since investigations have not been carried out to establish or refute either claim, they are as true as they are false. Their unsubstantiated status keeps them open to contestation, weakening particularly the claims of the marginalised. Moreover, frequent assertions by political leaders and the police that many of those who disappeared had sufficiently exercised their agency in separating from their families are particularly damaging. Such disinformation puts half-widows and their children at risk of re-traumatisation and renders them vulnerable to a heightened sense of abandonment. By advocating and insisting on legitimising this statist narrative, half-widows become victims of not the crime of enforced disappearance but of betrayal by their spouses, something that is apolitical in statist terms.

By promoting this view, the state is able to do three things: first, it denies the fact that many of those who are 'reportedly missing' were victims of a crime; second, following the dismissal of the crime, the victimhood of half-widows and their families is also dismissed; third, this narrative helps the government to absolve itself of the responsibility to carry out elaborate investigations to establish culpability, which would raise questions about securitisation and militarism.

One of the ways in which impunity is entrenched in the Valley is through the overvaluation of the 'official' or statist truth claim as the one to which more legitimacy can be justifiably accorded. However, since no data backs these assertions, unknowability creates an irresolvable quandary. The problem of unknowability only props up the state's truth claims: the public is furnished misinformation regarding disappearances with little recourse to gaining access to information that has not been tampered with in the service of purported national security and national interest. This enables opposing logics against national security to lose their credibility. Sustaining conditions of unknowability helps the contentions of dissenters – who dispute the need for militarism – to be frequently claimed as unfounded in the larger public discourse overwhelmingly taken with the logic of national security. This evidences the need for the importance of the problem of unknowability as a viable political tool to advance national security interests, and to resist the scourge of the international community on rampant rights violations as a governance strategy in the Valley.

Article 24 of the Convention on the Protection of All Persons from Enforced Disappearance, which India has signed but not ratified, clearly states, 'each victim has the right to know the truth regarding the circumstances of the enforced disappearance, the progress and results of the investigation and the fate of the disappeared person' (International Convention for the Protection of All Persons from Enforced Disappearance, 2007, 12). Not only has the Indian state not provided any information on those who were made to disappear but it has also refused to acknowledge the victimhood of persons affected by the crime, and instead furnished questionable, unverified information about 'missing' persons adding to the Valley's incertitude. Over time the crime of enforced disappearance has created many perpetrators who have been responsible for intensifying the violence suffered by half-widows. Such individuals have actively denied half-widows' access to remedies, spread misinformation, discredited their narratives and refused to accommodate their fears and misgivings into the justice system.

The problem of justice faced by half-widows needs to be firmly situated in the context of institutional and structural failings, understood as violence by the Indian state, that reduce them to, what Giorgio Agamben calls, 'bare lives' (Agamben, 2005). Drawing from Agamben, Lauren Wilcox argues that 'national security states' often 'de-politicise life, rendering it a biological proposition of avoiding death' (Wilcox, 2015, 25). Survival is made to compete with justice, wherein the latter can always be vulnerable to the privileging of the former. The starkest example of this is probably in the ex gratia relief payment that half-widows can obtain, albeit at a price. The cost of obtaining it is the declaration of death of their 'missing' husbands. This flawed reparations scheme demands that half-widows abandon the fight for justice, which many are unwilling to do (Bhattacharya, 2016, 80). But since these women are mostly unskilled and illiterate, struggling to barely make ends meet, the payment is attractive. The conditional reparations scheme, unfair and unjust as it is, makes it hard for half-widows to accept money from the state without a serious moral dilemma: either accept the money and recover from destitution or struggle for justice and fight harder for sustenance. However, it is worth noting here that the ex gratia relief payment itself is not designated for half-widows; its legitimate claimants can only be women who are willing to be identified as widows by agreeing with the state's presumption of their husband's death. In such cases, unknowability can be resolved in a manner that helps the state escape accountability as conditions of death would remain unknown in the absence of the body and the push for justice.

The state's national security logic allows it the power to perform violent forms of misrecognition which leads to these disappearances, so the fact that the state does not legally recognise it as crime does not come across as surprising. As members of the security forces continue to exercise their free will in Kashmir, an enabling environment is sustained wherein justice is continually denied and information withheld or distorted and victims are never recognised as such. The non-recognition of the crime is linked to militarisation, which adds to the vulnerability of half-widows who have become victims of not only the crime of enforced disappearance but also the preponderance of the logic of national security advocated by the state. The narratives of half-widows are marginalised in the dominant public discourse in India because acknowledging the cause of their suffering would contribute to asking uncomfortable questions about the state, military governance and a democratic shortfall in Kashmir, and would implicate large sections of state and security forces. Unknowability has its merits in keeping this from happening and has hence flourished despite its many injustices.

Violence of injustice and national security politics

In Kashmir, security forces either undertook joint operations with the Jammu and Kashmir police or detained people by themselves. Many were arrested from their homes or village of residence during house searches and had family members or neighbours as witnesses to confirm it. Many were also picked up from public places where eyewitnesses abound (Farasat, 2014, 87). Farasat (2014) argues that

> in any criminal offence these details are enough to start a process of investigation and filing of charge sheets based on preliminary enquiry by the police. However, in none of these cases were the accused produced before criminal courts to face trial.
>
> (88)

This leads us to an understanding of impunity, which 'conveys not only the lack of legal remedies available to individual victims, but also the failure of democratic institutions to respond to egregious crimes' (Farasat, 2014, 97). Even as juridical institutions exist and promise accountability and redress through their mere existence, a vicious cycle of cover-up and denial infests the legal system which leads to the denial of justice and the perpetuation of military control, making the law appear to be a sham (Duschinski and Hoffman, 2011, 46). Neera Chhandoke (2010) argues that injustices can be remedied if individuals are able to access the judiciary, if democracy is effective and if civil society organisations are able to put pressure on governments to address injustices.

However, none of these conditions has been adequately met in the Valley. Chhandoke (2010) argues that reinstating democracy through the scrapping of coercive laws is challenging and increases the risk of subversion. Moreover, civil society actors are also frequently swayed 'by the official dismissal of the struggle in the Valley as terrorism, and as the handiwork of neighbouring countries, and far too many agents have been prejudiced against militants by reasons of a corrosive nationalism, and a biased media' (Chhandoke, 2010, 62). This has further obstructed the path through which justice is to be sought for half-widows in the Valley.

Vittorio Bufacchi (2007) holds injustice to be a kind of violence (164). Drawing from John Stuart Mill's insights in *On Liberty*, Bufacchi's theorisation of violence by omission holds particular significance in the Kashmir context. Bufacchi argues that violence can be inflicted through an omission or inaction, and not necessarily through direct infliction of harm at all times. However, violence by omission carries significantly less moral weight than direct acts of violence. He categorises several ways in which omissions can cause violence. First, through omitted action, and second, through omitting action. The former refers to cases where violence occurs when no effort is made to prevent it. Violence by omitting action refers to cases whereby one action is done instead of another even when the former could have prevented violence. He then goes on to categorise omitting actions into negative action and negative causation. Negative action is pertinent to our understanding of Kashmir. It is not preventing violence despite knowledge of the consequences of inaction (Bufacchi, 2007, 50–51). The state has perpetuated violence through this kind of omitting action described by Bufacchi which has significant bearing on the lives of half-widows.

Security forces are allowed to function with impunity in Jammu and Kashmir despite having been known to perpetrate large-scale human rights violations and severely hinder the mobility and freedom of those fighting for justice. The security forces in Kashmir have indulged in crimes of enforced disappearances, unlawful killings and torture, and criminal intimidation. Security forces have also been known to perpetrate sexual atrocities against half-widows and victim families to punish them for demanding justice and muzzle voices of dissent. This follows from the presumed helplessness of these women whose primary male protector or husband is 'missing'. By doing this, not only is the victim intimidated but many fighting similar battles are dissuaded from resisting the state and voicing their grievances. The fact that security forces have indulged in violent excesses in the Valley is well known and thereby the knowledge of these forms of control and 'punishment' could keep these women from pursuing their objectives. Hence, the repeal of AFSPA and other repressive legislation is understood as necessary to restore faith in the justice system.

However, as members of the security forces continue to exercise their free will in Kashmir, an enabling environment is sustained wherein justice is continually denied and information withheld or distorted and victims are never recognised as such. The non-recognition of the crime is linked to militarisation and securitisation which together add to the vulnerability of half-widows because they are victims of not only the crime of enforced disappearance but also the preponderance of the logic of national security advocated by the state. Hence, justice becomes all the more difficult to deliver. The narratives of half-widows are marginalised in the dominant public discourse in India because the cause of their suffering can never be acknowledged or ascertained, as acknowledging their suffering would contribute to asking uncomfortable questions about the state and its security practices and politics, as well as military governance and a democratic shortfall in Kashmir.

Raising questions of justice would implicate state forces. The justice question of the half-widows in Kashmir is tied to the question of (in)security politics. According to Mohanty (2011), 'national security states or security regimes typically use connected strategies of militarisation, criminalisation and incarceration to exercise control over particular populations, thus remaking individual subjectivities and public culture' (77). This produces '"bio-militarised" bodies that live under a constant state of dispossession and with a lack of basic civil rights evident in the dissolution of citizenship in occupied or securitised zones' (Mohanty, 2011, 78). Dibyesh Anand (2012) likens the Indian state to a 'postcolonial informal empire', where centre–periphery relations are based on the minoritisation of 'borderland ethno-nationalist communities within the large nationalist project', and which has a centre that reluctantly accepts cultural difference and autonomy, but rejects any compromise on military and political control and denies political agency to the borderland minorities (73).

The violence, injustice and insecurity suffered by half-widows cannot be dissociated from the politics of national security. However, owing to the mainstream of IR's state-centric focus, such connections have not so far been explored, and the disempowerment of women, because of the particular conduct of the Indian state and its security politics, has not been problematised. This sustains precarity and conditions of injustice for half-widows who are forever waiting: waiting to be heard, provided with information and reparations, waiting to be granted their rights as citizens in the largest democracy that India believes itself to be.

Works cited

Agamben, G. (2005). *State of Exception*. Chicago: University of Chicago Press.

Agencies. (2012). 'Unmarked Graves: Rights Group asks SHRC for DNA Test'. *The Indian Express*. 30 August. http://archive.indianexpress.com/news/unmarked-graves-rights-group-asks-shrc-for-dna-test/995459/. Accessed 11 January 2019.

Anand, D. (2012). 'China and India: Postcolonial Informal Empires in the Emerging Global Order'. *Rethinking Marxism: A Journal of Economics, Culture & Society*, 24(1), 68–86.

Ashiq, P. (2012). 'APDP Submits 507 Cases of Disappearances to Kashmir SHRC'. *Hindustan Times*. 30 August. www.hindustantimes.com/india/apdp-submits-507-cases-of-disappearances-to-kashmir-shrc/story-mkqQKjjuGVwKD1erco3SkK.html. Accessed 11 January 2019.

Association of Parents of Disappeared Persons (APDP) (2011). 'Half-Widow, Half Wife?: Responding to Gender Violence in Kashmir'. July. https://kafilabackup.files.wordpress.com/2011/07/half-widow-half-wife-apdp-report.pdf. Accessed 11 January 2019.

Bashir, A. (2011). 'Kashmir's Half-Widows Shoulder the Burden of a Double Tragedy'. *The Guardian*. 11 October. www.theguardian.com/global-development/2010/oct/11/1. Accessed 11 January 2019.

Behera, N.C. (2006). *Demystifying Kashmir*. Washington, DC: Brookings Institution Press.

Bhattacharya, D. (2016). *The Plight of Kashmiri Half-Widows*, Policy Report No. 16. New Delhi: The Hindu Centre for Politics and Public Policy.
Bose, S. (2009). *Kashmir: Roots of Conflict, Paths to Peace*. Cambridge, MA: Harvard University Press.
Bose, T., Mohan, D., Navlakha, G. and Banerjee, S. (1990). 'India's "Kashmir War"'. *Economic and Political Weekly*, 25(13), 650–662.
Bufacchi, V. (2007). *Violence and Social Justice*. New York: Palgrave Macmillan.
Bukhari, S. (2011). 'DNA Profiling on Bodies in J&K Graves to Begin'. *The Hindu*, 27 September. www.thehindu.com/news/DNA-profiling-on-bodies-in-J&K-graves-to-begin/article13613643.ece. Accessed 11 January 2019.
Chatterjee, A.P. (2011). 'The Militarised Zone'. In: T. Ali, H. Bhatt, A.P. Chatterjee, H. Khatun, P. Mishra, and A. Roy (eds.) *Kashmir: The Case for Freedom*. New York: Verso, pp. 93–124.
Chengappa, B.M. (2000). 'The ISI Role in Pakistan's Politics'. *Strategic Analysis*, 23(11), 1857–1878.
Chhandoke, N. (2010). 'When Is Secession Justified? The Context of Kashmir'. *Economic and Political Weekly*, 45(46), 59–66.
D'Souza, P. (2016). 'Life-as-Lived Today: Perpetual (Undesired) Liminality of the Half-Widows of Kashmir'. *Culture Unbound: Journal of Current Cultural Research*, 8, 26–42.
Duschinski, H. and B. Hoffman (2011). 'Everyday Violence, Institutional Denial and Struggles for Justice in Kashmir'. *Race and Class*, 52(4), 44–70.
Enloe, C. (1996). 'Margins, Silences, and Bottom Rungs: How to Overcome the Underestimation of Power in the Study of International Relations'. In: S. Smith, K. Booth and M. Zalewski (eds.) *International Theory: Positivism and Beyond*. Cambridge: Cambridge University Press, pp. 186–202.
Farasat, W. (2014). 'Examining Justice and Accountability in Kashmir'. In: P. Hoeing and N. Singh (eds.) *Landscapes of Fear: Understanding Impunity in India*. New Delhi: Zubaan, pp. 73–109.
Ganguly, S. (1996). 'Explaining the Kashmir Insurgency: Political Mobilisation and Institutional Decay'. *International Security*, 21(2), 76–107.
Gregory, S. (2007). 'The ISI and the War on Terrorism'. *Studies in Conflict and Terrorism*, 30(12), 1014.
Human Rights Watch (2011). 'India: Investigate Unmarked Graves in Jammu and Kashmir'. 24 August. www.hrw.org/news/2011/08/24/india-investigate-unmarked-graves-jammu-and-kashmir. Accessed 11 January 2019.
IANS. (2015). 'The Pain of Dardpora: Kashmiri Half-Widows Living in a State of Limbo'. *Business Standard*. 6 October. https://www.business-standard.com/article/news-ians/the-pain-of-dardpora-kashmiri-half-widows-living-in-a-state-of-limbo-115100600451_1.html. Accessed 11 January 2019.
Kazi, S. (2014). 'Rape, Impunity and Justice in Kashmir'. *Socio-Legal Review*, 10, 14–46.
Kazi, S. (2015). 'South Asia's Gendered "War on Terror"'. In: R. Baksh and W. Harcourt (eds.) *The Oxford Handbook of Transnational Feminist Movements*. New York: Oxford University Press, pp. 668–698.
Mohanty, C.T. (1991). 'Under Western Eyes: Feminist Scholarship and Colonial Discourse'. In: C.T. Mohanty, A. Russo and L. Torres (eds.) *Third World Women and the Politics of Feminism*. Bloomington, IN: Indiana University Press, pp. 51–80.
Mohanty, C.T. (2011). 'Imperial Democracies, Militarised Zones, Feminist Engagements'. *Economic and Political Weekly*, 46(13), 76–84.

Mohanty, C.T., A. Russo and L. Torres (eds.) (1991). *Third World Women and the Politics of Feminism*. Bloomington, IN: Indiana University Press.

Navlakha, G. (2002). 'Security Policy: Enemy of Democracy'. *Economic and Political Weekly*, 37(33), 3420–3428.

Olapally, D.M. (2008). *The Politics of Extremism in South Asia*. New York: Cambridge University Press.

Parashar, S., J.A. Tickner and J. True (2018). 'Introduction: Feminist Imaginings of Twenty-First-Century Gendered States'. In: S. Parashar, J.A. Tickner and J. True (eds.) *Revisiting Gendered States: Feminist Imaginings of the State in International Relations*. New York: Oxford University Press, pp. 1–18.

Parthasarathy, S. (2016). 'The Plight of Kashmir's Half-Widows and Widows'. *The Wire*. 28 June. https://thewire.in/politics/the-plight-of-kashmirs-half-widows-and-widows. Accessed 11 January 2019.

Qutab, S. (2012). 'Women Victims of Armed Conflict: Half-Widows in Jammu and Kashmir'. *Sociological Bulletin*, 61(2), 255–278.

Scott, D. (2011). 'India's Relations with Pakistan'. In: D. Scott (ed.) *Handbook of India's International Relations*. London: Routledge, pp. 59–69.

Scott, D. (ed.) (2011). *Handbook of India's International Relations*. London: Routledge.

Special Correspondent (2011). 'J&K Human Rights Commission's SIT Confirms, 2156 Unidentified Bodies in "Mass Graves"'. *The Hindu*. 22 August. https://www.thehindu.com/news/national/jk-human-rights-commissions-sit-confirms-2156-unidentified-bodies-in-mass-graves/article2379921.ece. Accessed 11 January 2019.

Umar, B. (2013). 'The Dilemma of Kashmir's Half-Widows'. *Al Jazeera*. 12 October. www.aljazeera.com/news/asia/2013/09/dilemma-kashmir-half-widows-201392715575877378.html. Accessed 11 January 2019.

United Nations Human Rights: Office of the High Commissioner. International Convention for the Protection of All Persons from Enforced Disappearance. https://www.ohchr.org/en/hrbodies/ced/pages/conventionced.aspx

Wilcox, L. (2015). *Bodies of Violence: Theorising Embodied Subjects in International Relations*. New York: Oxford University Press.

Winchell, S.P. (2003). 'Pakistan's ISI: The Invisible Government'. *International Journal of Intelligence and CounterIntelligence*, 16(3), 374–388.

3 The RSS's 'Village Republics'

Rakesh Ankit

> Mullah ko Jo hai Hind mein Sajde ki Ijazat
> Nadan ye Samajhta hai ke Islam hai Azad
> – Allama Iqbal
> (In India, if bare leave be deigned his prayer-prostration,
> Our dull priest thinks Islam has gained emancipation)

Allama Iqbal died in 1938. This chapter offers an ethnographic analysis of how, in the *Hind* of 2018, a spectre hangs over public prayer by ordinary Muslims. It sets out a 'familiar storyline involving a disputed mosque and claims of harassment of women' (Apoorvanand, Ali Javed and Satish Deshpande, 2015). Specifically, attention is focused on a small village of around 500 families called Devru/ Dewarhu. In April 2016, Devru/Dewarhu was reported as 'another Ayodhya in the making' (Bhardwaj, 2016). In conjunction with colleagues working at the nearby O.P. Jindal Global University, I visited Devru on 24 April and 1 May 2016, not so much to collect 'facts' as to confirm our forebodings and fears that Devru forms part of a pattern that is starting to take shape in recent times: a *Hindu Rashtra* is on the make in India, village by village – from Atali to Bishara to Jhabar (Yadav, *The Dadri Lynching and Jharkhand*, 2015). *Village* has long been considered an 'entry-point' of the Indian nation (Jodhka, 2002). Established as 'India-in-microcosm', it was essentialised in the colonial period as 'village republic' and eulogised by Gandhi as 'a site of authenticity' (Jodhka, 2002).

Located off the National Highway 1 near the town of Sonipat in Haryana, Devru is a part of the Municipal Corporation of Sonipat and neighbours the upscale sectors 14 and 15 of Haryana Urban Development Authority (HUDA). The sitting MLA, Kavita Jain and MP of the area, Ramesh Kaushik, reside in these sectors. Between 150 and 175 Muslim families live in Devru today. A large number of these are from the Jat caste and are called Muley/Mola/Mula Jats. Some have come from the nearby Uttar Pradesh (UP), and these 'unstable social labels' were our entry points into their 'displaced histories' (Stoler, 2010). The majority of Hindus in the village are from castes that comprise the Scheduled and Other Backward Castes categories. The 'head' of the Muslims in Devru is Hajji Jumma. Born in 1956, Jumma performed the Hajj in 2002 and is a local figure respected by Muslims and non-Muslims alike as reflected in his successive victories in *Panchayat* elections in 2000 and 2005. He is a descendant of 1 of the 13 families left behind in Devru in the aftermath of post-Partition violence in this area in September 1947. They, alongside others who 'stayed, constituting ten percent of population', had to answer the question: 'Can a Muslim really be an Indian ... one of the enduring legacies of Partition, [which has] to do with the way in which the Indian state [has] gone about the task of managing "difference"' (Pandey, 1999). Through their words, this chapter seeks to convey a slice of the 'social imaginaries' and 'emotional economies' (Stoler, 2010) underneath.

I

From the late 1940s to the mid-1960s, the old and now dilapidated village mosque, abandoned since 1980 and the site of the current dispute, served as a shelter for Hindu refugees from Pakistan and earned the sobriquet '*Rihayashi Masjid*' (Residential Mosque). On 1 April 1965, in response to a petition filed by the Muslims of Devru, the Sonipat Civil Court accepted it as a mosque, handed it over to the State Waqf Board (bodies set-up by State Governments under the Waqf Act, 1954 to look after religious properties) and ordered the evacuation of its residents. As Hajji Jumma put it, however, '*Masjid maan li gayi par khali nahin Hui*' (It was accepted as a mosque but was not vacated). This defiance on the part of local Hindus against the court's order and this inability of local Muslims to benefit from it can be contextualised within the withdrawal of 'Muslims from the public sphere' in India in the years following Partition. Devru is located in what was then East Punjab, from where Muslims were expelled *en masse*. Those who stayed, like the 13 families in Devru, have been said to have 'adopted Hinduism. They changed their culture, names and customs.' It has been read as another example of India's 'unity in diversity' and Devru 'being home to an unusual variety of Islam today' (Bhardwaj, 2016). Such a reading ignores the 'incorporative violence' by which the Muslims in India were sought to be 'internalise[d] within the emerging national order', a process that transformed India's Muslims from a 'national' political community to a religious 'minority' (Purushotham, 2015).

Purushotham's analysis is borne out in the sentiments expressed by Hajji Jumma. As he put it, '*dehshat mein Musalman, Musalman nahin rahe*' (In fear, Muslims did not remain as Muslims). Names like *Manglu* (born on *Mangal* – Tuesday) and *Jumma* (born on *Jumma* – Friday) were kept, *Namaaz* was offered at home and daughters were offered in marriage to the Hindus. That this ought not to be read as 'conversion' is clear by the fact that from mid-1970s, as some sense of security returned, Muslims started offering *Namaaz* at the village *chaupal* (square), started sending their children to the village school and started practising endogamy; that this was not an attempt at 'syncretism' either is established by the fact that despite discarding their 'Muslim-ness' they were never entirely accepted by the Hindus of the village, a point made tellingly by the Hindus through their refusal to marry their daughters into Muslim families. Meanwhile, the occupied mosque started to become a source of contention and it was only in 1980 that Hindu families vacated the mosque in pursuance of the Sonipat Civil Court's April 1965 order.

This, however, proved to be the first page of a new chapter of discord. In the mid-1980s, tensions emerged as the Hindus resorted to conducting *kirtans* and putting up calendars with Hindu gods on the walls of the mosque in a bid to signal their continuing control over the site. In 1985, after one particularly tense period, under section 145 of the criminal procedure code, the building was sealed. In the local *Thana*, a mutual negotiation was sought but the Hindus did not agree and took their case to the Sessions District Magistrate (SDM), who ruled in their favour. Ignoring the 1965 decision, the SDM argued that the site had been 'used as a temple'. This illustration of 'possession being 9/10th of the law' can be understood within paradigms as different as the north Indian vernacular epithet '*jiski lathi, uski bhains*' (might is right) and Mikhail Bakhtin's term, 'heteroglossia'. This was a case of the state (judiciary) and the society (Hindus in the village) putting together a dialogic intersection of contradictory jargons and languages to produce a meaning quite different from the sum of the parts (Robinson, 2011). To understand quite what this meaning could be, we need to approach it through Quentin Skinner and his ideas of 'intentionality' and 'illocutionary force'. Skinner wrote that while 'the illocutionary acts we perform are identified, like all voluntary acts, by our intentions; the illocutionary forces carried by our utterances are mainly determined by their meaning and context' (cited in McCullough, 2002).

In order to perceive this proposition of a mosque being 'used as a temple', its wider sense needs to be remembered. Authorial intentions, motivations and convictions, in this case those of the judge, need to be contextualised and interpreted within the worsening communal climate of Devru, Haryana and India of the mid-1980s – with the rise of the *Ram Janmabhoomi Movement* (Blom Hansen, 1999). This accelerated communalisation of Indian political and civil society was reflected in an increasing convergence of the *Vishwa Hindu Parishad*-led Ram Janmabhoomi Movement, on the one hand, and the then-ruling Congress Party's increasing pandering to Hindu nationalism as illustrated by 'Prime Minister Indira Gandhi's blessings to the Kalash Yatra and Rajiv Gandhi's "Ram Raj" speech at Ayodhya and support given to the *shilanyas*' (Panikkar, 1990). The argument given there was familiar: 'The Muslims have to understand. They cannot build their mosque at the disputed site ... Should they not follow their religion and leave this disputed place?' (Apoorvanand and Deshpande, 2015). What it produced in Ayodhya was the demolition of the Babri Masjid in December 1992, while in Devru it caused a physical deterioration of the structure visible today. Neither was it used as a temple nor was it allowed to be used as a mosque. At the same time, in keeping with the winds blowing in *Ram ke Naam* in north India (Patwardhan, 1992), a village that had not one temple in modern memory saw the construction of four, with Muslims contributing both labour and capital.

Disillusioned by the judgement of the SDM, the Muslims began to construct a madrassa in 1987–88 on a space adjoining the disputed structure. Inevitably, there was an objection to this construction but, once valid documents were produced, the SDM let it proceed. The madrassa was built largely from the revenue that came from the nine acres of agricultural land that was in the name of the old mosque, outside the village. In 1995, the Waqf laid claim to this land. Muslims of Devru, incensed at the Waqf's inability to restore to them the village mosque, objected and filed a case in the Punjab and Haryana High Court on 29 April 2005. Hajji Jumma, then *Sarpanch* of Devru, led this attempt to challenge the Waqf's authority. He was distraught at this dual '*tauhini of Islam*' (insult of Islam): first, at the hands of Hindus and then at the Waqf's inability to take possession of the disputed site under the 1965 judgement, combined with its claim of the agricultural land. He would have let the Waqf have the land outside the village, if the Waqf had got them the mosque. And so his position vis-à-vis both the Waqf and the Hindus on the agricultural land outside and the disputed site inside was the same: '*hamaari cheez hai, unki kya?*' (It is ours; nothing to them). Even the High Court was moved in October 2008 to remind the negligent Waqf that despite nearly 170 Muslim families living in Devru, there was no place of prayer for them. It instructed the Waqf to renovate the old mosque, by now in a terrible condition. Citing shortage of funds, the Waqf told the Muslims to do it on their own.

II

This local flashpoint got enmeshed into the larger political milieu in 2015. Three back-to-back events – victory of the Bharatiya Janata Party (BJP)-led National Democratic Alliance in the 2014 general election, the BJP's win in the Haryana state election subsequently and Devru's incorporation into the jurisdiction of the Municipal Corporation of Sonipat – provide an immediate backdrop to the current crisis. The first two represent the bitter fruits of the historical roots of Hindu nationalism in modern India: the overlapping/concentric relationship between the so-called 'secular' Congress nationalism and the *Sangh Parivar*'s 'Hindu' nationalism: a relationship of similar essence if different emphasis (van der Veer, 1994). As shown recently by William Gould and Akshaya Mukul for neighbouring Uttar Pradesh (UP), the language used by political operators of the Congress contained references to 'Hindu-ness', rhetoric about the catholicity of Hinduism and rationale about its ability to embrace in its fold other religions, thereby resulting in an exclusionary posture towards non-Hindus (Gould, 2004; Mukul, 2015). Connections at the local level between Congress and various Hindu organisations, notably the Mahasabha and the Arya Samaj, institutions, chiefly temples, and events, like *melas*, contributed to its image as a party with strong 'Hindu' roots (Maclean, 2008). 'Hinduism' was so ingrained in Congress's imagery and iconography by the 1940s that it prepared the ground for both the 'militarisation' of the Hindus and the 'minoritisation' of the Muslims. From there, as Perry Anderson (2013) put it, 'the success of [BJP] was due not just to the faltering of the [Congress], but to their ability to articulate openly what had always been latent … but neither candidly acknowledged, nor consistently repudiated.'

In Devru, the pretext for this was the desire of the Muslims to construct an *Id-gah*, a prayer wall, on some of the land that the old mosque owned outside the village. While the local police station quickly termed it an illegal construction, the local *Rashtriya Swayamsevak Sangh* (RSS estd. 1925) *shakha*, reportedly, started spreading baseless rumours like '*Id-gah ke bajai gai kaatne ki jagah banai ja rahi hai*' (Not an *Id-gah* but a slaughter house for cows is being constructed). There was much tension in the months of July–August–September 2015. The superintendent of police (SP) asked the Hajji if they had sought permission to build the prayer wall. An incredulous Hajji shot back, 'What for? Why should we ask for permission when the land is ours?' The SP then pressured the Waqf to step in and stop the building of the *Id-gah*; the Waqf resisted by citing the pending HC case. Tensions reached a fever pitch between 24 and 27 September with much stone-pelting and people from both sides leaving the village. Representatives of both sides were summoned by the local police on the 28th. Meanwhile, some random charges were registered on some Muslims, which were later proved to be false.

When Hajji Jumma turned up for the meeting, he found non-village, assumably, RSS persons/collaborators sitting with the *Tehsildar* and faced a call to break down the *Id-gah* wall. As he refused this '*naajayaz dabane ki baat*' (illegal–immoral imposition), the conversation coalesced around two things: Waqf versus Muslims on the *Id-gah* land and Hindus versus Muslims on the old mosque site. Harassed, the Hajji conceded a compromise by which the Hindus promised to refrain from any action on the *Id-gah* in return for the construction of a community hall on the disputed site. In his six decades in India, Hajji Jumma had never seen such an '*ektarfa*' police (one-sided) debate. Equally, as a former, popularly elected *Sarpanch*, he was pained to note that the economically poor and socially backward groups had been so easily pushed to the forefront of the *Id-gah* conflagration by a promise of '*sau-sau gaz zameen*' (a hundred square metres of land) to be parcelled from the *Id-gah* land. That the Dalit, historically oppressed by caste Hindus, could so easily be turned anti-Muslim by them, led likely by the RSS workers/supporters, conducting evening meetings and temple visits, came as a shock to him. At the heart of this socio-religious compromise extracted from the Hajji remains the unease that surrounds Muslims as a 'political category' in India since Partition (Purushotham, 2015).

As the local MLA, Kavita Jain, descended on Devru in early April 2016 to lay the foundation stone of the community hall, not one Muslim attended the ceremony. Jain, ironically the state minister for Social Justice and Empowerment, Women and Child Development, shot back to questioning journalists, insolently, 'it may have been a mosque before independence. That does not make it a mosque today' ('Fear Grips Muslims', 2016). For Muslims, this capped the phase of provocations in the name of processions in 2015 – no fewer than six – all of which had been accompanied by the police and had seen stone-pelting, sloganeering, sword and *lathi* wielding and flag-waving in front of the madrassa. The Hajji put it ominously, '*who to ek tarfa khamoshi thi, warna qatl-e-aam ho jata*' (But for our one-sided silence, there would have been blood). With one *swayamsevak* as prime minister of the country and another as chief minister of the state, little wonder that in villages like Devru, the RSS workers and other like-minded Hindus have never had it so good. After all, to quote Anderson (2013), 'official secularity is not meaningless. If India is a confessional state, it is by default, not prescription.' In this darkening sky, the Jat agitation for OBC reservation in the months of February and March 2016 came as an unlikely silver lining for these

Muley/Mola/Mula Jats. As the state and society in Haryana got diverted by this larger issue, the Hajji breathed a relative sigh of relief, '*pind chuta Jat aarakshan aandolan se*' (The Jat agitation got the monkey off our backs). In the wake of the agitation, Muley/Mola/Mula Jats were one of the subcategories, among Jats, to be granted an OBC status.

If the absence of physical violence signals normalcy, then the situation in Devru is 'normal', but for the Muslims there, as in most of India, it is a 'new' normal: an uneasy present always tinged with a fear of the future. As Apoorvanand observed in the case of the Atali violence, 'they feel trapped. They live with the acute awareness that there is no support for them in a hostile Hindu neighbourhood and village' (Apoorvanand [sic], Javed and Deshpande, 2015). So is the case with Devru. This sense of seclusion can be gauged from the matter-of-fact reply that the Hajji gave to a query about the nearest Muslim village, Tharra – four to five kilometres away – populated by Gujjar Muslims: a prosperous, entrenched and secure mini-world with three mosques and a madrassa in the village but with little interaction with their Devru co-religionists. Nor could any sense of expectations or belied hopes be detected from the Hajji's demeanour. Nobody seemed to have come from Tharra in solidarity during July–September 2015 and nobody from Devru seemed to have left for Tharra for refuge.

There is a psychological violence and sense of victimhood that pervades Devru's Muslims. All 'outside' visitors to them – from their relatives to us, university tutors – are unfailingly reported to the local *Thanedar*, who threateningly asks, 'Why are people coming?' Never had the Hajji had such a sense of separateness of hearts and minds in his 50 years in Devru. Visible signs of this separateness are the prominent *Om* and *Swastika* symbols painted on every non-Muslim house by the RSS workers (Bhardwaj, 2016; 'Fear Grips Muslims', 2016). These markings bode ill in case of impending violence and are an overt, for covert it always was, demonstration of the hegemonic Hindu in ascendance and arrogance. There is now little but perfunctory interaction between the two sides in the village including among the elderly and the children. As the Hajji put it, '*khataas aa gayi hai*' (Relations are bitter]. As Apoorvanand despaired upon his return from Atali, so there was a similar despondency in Devru:

> Is this the future of India – a state of permanent fear and tension for religious, ethnic, caste, or linguistic minorities bullied by an intolerant majority, egged on by venal politicians and ineffective [complicit] state machinery?
> (Apoorvanand [sic], Javed and Deshpande, 2015)

III

If such is the social mood; what of the expectations from the state? There remains a hope for justice; after all, the 'permanent stay' granted by the Civil Court on the community hall is the latest and the strongest crutch for them to lean on. There remains a belief in the justness of their stand but they have no faith in the judiciary. Who can blame them? For the way the courts and the police have behaved, periodically since 1985, has introduced a 'fear factor': the very thing the latter is meant to eradicate. That there is nothing but a naked majoritarianism upholstering this fear is illuminated by a sharp question that the Hajji asks, 'has there ever been a temple claimed by the Muslims in India as their own?' As for that amorphous thing called the media, the Devru Muslims are caught in a bind. They do not have a network in that ecosystem and yet publicity for their cause is priceless for them. When times were bad, not one media person/outlet came to report and the recent, limited coverage had only been in the wake of, and, ironically, at the behest of the laying of the foundation stone by the local MLA. The other side cannot be more alive to this, for the local *Thanedar* regularly calls the Hajji and warns him, '*Media-walloh ko gaon mein naa aane do; gaon ka maahaul kharab hota hai*' (Do not let media persons come inside the village; the atmosphere vitiates).

Lest they forget, as articulated by a younger one: '*Aaj Hindustan mein Muslim ko Mujrim banane ki koshish ki jaa rahi hai, Media mein*' (In India today, the media treats Muslims as criminals). With no political patronage – '*Sarkar unka saath de rahi hai*' (Government is supporting them), slim legal hopes – '*Insaaf nahin*' (no justice), and no presence in the regional state apparatus – not a single Muslim of Devru has a government job – they are a beleaguered lot. In this they share their fate with millions of their co-religionists in India. In 2006, the Justice Rajinder Sachar Commission reported that of the roughly 138 million Muslims then in India, 13.4% of the population, not more than 5% were in government service of any hue (Anderson, 2013). As for the judiciary, a popular adage summed up their situation, punning on the acronym *ADALAT* (court), '*Aao, daava karo, lado, tabaah ho jao*' (Come, claim, fight and get destroyed in the process). In September 1947, ten trucks came to Devru from the nearby Rohtak refugee camp to take Muslims to Pakistan. Hajji Jumma's family did not board the trucks as his uncle was away just then. When the grandfather of another elderly Muslim was offered a princely Rs. 1000 for his land, he pithily replied, '*Saari zindagi to yahan jiye hain, ab marne ke liye wahan kya jayenge*' (Lived all our life here, why go there only to die?). Such are the slender yet simple reasons that throw some light on the 13 Muslim families who stayed in Devru. Seventy years of a life of economic labour – on their agricultural land; social exclusion – as India's 'internal other'; and political exploitation – as a 'vote-bank' has yielded them and their descendants charges of disloyalty. As one noted with anguish:

> *Phool the, Talwaar kehlaye hum; Zakhm khakar bhi Sitamgar kehlaye hum*
> *Saari qurbani Raigaah ho gayi; Jaan dekar bhi Gaddaar kehlaye hum*
> (Flower we were but were called Sword; Victim we were but were called Oppressor
> All our Sacrifice went in Vain; despite giving our Lives we were called Traitor)

Allama Iqbal saw it coming. Muslims of India have never had a more valid *Shikwa* (complaint) to make than today when under the baton of the RSS, there is a *Hindu Rashtra* on the make, village by village – from Atali to Bishara (The Dadri

Lynching, 2015) to Jhabar (Pandey, 2016), to Devru. And, this *Hindu Rashtra* celebrates a *Gramotsav* (village festival) with the slogan '*Gaam Raam hota hai*' (village is where Lord Ram is); a case of 'performative politics' laying bare the lack of any place in it for Hajji Jumma (Kaur, 2003). After all, as Ambedkar put it, 'the Hindu village is the working plant of the Hindu social order' (Jodhka 2002), and, as this coda of observer commentary shows, it feeds those 'sensory regimes by which people distinguish "we" from "they"' (Stoler, 2010). Organised by the RSS, the fifth instalment of this annual ritual, inaugurated by *Sarsanghkaryavahak* Suresh Joshi in 2014, was recently held in the village of Bhali Anandpur, located off the National Highway 10, in the district of Rohtak in Haryana, on 25 February 2018. It was attended by the state labour minister, Nayab Singh Saini. Upon arrival, at this exercise in social engineering, the first thing that was striking was the overlap with the state apparatus. Amongst those present were a serving constable of Delhi Police, a retired honorary officer (veterinarian) of the Indian Army, a union civil service candidate who had cleared a state public service examination, a number of teachers from government colleges/schools and most members of the District Board and village *Panchayat*. This illustrated what Omar Khalidi titled 'Hinduising India: secularism in practice' (2008), which had shown empirically that 'far from being a state practising neutrality or equidistance from all religions, the Indian state is directly involved in Hinduisation of the country … *regardless of the party in power.*'

This is especially striking today in light of the current 'acceptance of the Political Hindu' (Raychaudhuri, 2017), reflected from the present prime minister downwards. Secondly, the merchandise on display there provided another kaleidoscope of the material commerce and human connection prevalent in the RSS's Village Republic. Prominent among these were ayurveda products and advertisements for examination-related coaching and computer training, juxtaposing the essence of modern services with the emblem of ancient wisdom. Next to them was *Atal Seva Kendra* (service centre), remembering former Prime Minister Atal Bihari Vajpayee and offering services for paperwork imperative in India today: *Aadhaar* (unique identification) and Permanent Account Number (PAN) cards. A utensils stall, of products made of locally available clay and locally manufactured, followed, next to which was an agricultural shed containing Vedic fertiliser. A nearby veterinary hospital's booth, with cut-outs of different breeds of cows, buffaloes and goats and their vaccination routines completed this agro-economic–educational complex, icons for which came from the stands of the Dr B.R. Ambedkar Library and the Vivekananda Club.

A survey of this particular combination of 'religious political parties and their welfare work' (Nair, 2009), was broken by the sounds of *mantras* being chanted around a fire-pit to give an auspicious start to the day. Led by priests from the Arya Samaj, carrying forward the legacy of their 19th-century Arya Dharm predecessors of curating 'Hindu Consciousness' in this region (Jones, 1976), it was approaching climax. Meanwhile, the stage was ready with the familiar portraits of the RSS's founder K.B. Hedgewar (1889–1940), his successor

M.S. Golwalkar (1906–1973) and *Mother India*, but also with two unfamiliar photographs of young men in Indian Navy and Air Force uniforms, later revealed as Naval officer Atul Pawar and Air Force pilot Sandeep and revered as '*gaon ke Shaheed*' (martyrs of the village). This 'convergence of maps, mothers/goddesses, and martyrdom' transforms nationalism–territorialism into 'a tangible and enduring object deemed deserving of the bodily sacrifice of the citizenry' (Ramaswamy, 2008). Their utilisation 'as a medium of representation' during 'political and memorial functions' depicts the *Shaheed* (martyr) so as to 'reawaken memories among the public of forgotten martyrs' (Copeman, 2013).

IV

The first of the song–dance routines tapped into regional identity and provincial pride. If the neighbouring UP is called the 'heartland' of the Indian nation (Kudaisya, 2006), then Haryana is often represented as its *Jatland* – named after its preponderant peasant group with their 'militaristic masculinities' (Chowdhry, 2013). As groups of colourfully dressed school-children started to perform popular Haryanvi songs, I slotted myself next to a young adult from the village, who was studying via a distance education college programme in Rohtak. A defence services aspirant, '*bhatere lagte hain gaon se*' (Many get in from the village), he had been a RSS *shakha*-goer since childhood, '*sab bachche jaate hain gaon se*' (All children from the village attend). He liked going there for '*manoranjan*' (entertainment), a point demonstrated unforgettably in the film *The Boy in the Branch* (1993) by filmmaker Lalit Vachani, who documented and summarised 'the stories and the games, the rituals and the play that socialise the young' (IMDb). Speaking fondly of the efforts of the local RSS, he intoned that the football ground we were sitting on had been built by it and girls of the village play there, in uniforms provided by it. Right on cue, there was an announcement from the stage that thanks to the '*Divya Sangathan*' (divine organisation) RSS, in Bhali Anandpur, '*har beti khel rahi hai, har beta padh raha hai*' (Every daughter is playing, every son is studying), thereby turning it into a '*Punya Bhoomi*' (Holy Land) that will produce more personas like freedom-fighters Bhagat Singh and Subhas Chandra Bose. This appropriation and invocation of all but India's first Prime Minister Jawaharlal Nehru is the telltale sign of the trajectories of nationalism and regionalism that the RSS is trailing under the theme of '*Samajik Kriya*'; the catch-all 'provision of social welfare services' (Nair, 2009). This *Gramotsav* itself was, formally, being organised by a *Shaheed* Chandrasekhar Azad *Samiti* thus tapping into existing channels of emotional resonance.

Meanwhile, tiny tots dressed in army fatigues mounted the stage and began a military march to the tune of a song, '*Vardi hai Bhagwan, Fauji mera Naam*' (Uniform is God, Soldier is my name), from the 1976 film *Fauji* (Soldier). Cheered on by a group of colourfully dressed girls – the limit of female participation in this political celebration of 'armed masculinity' and 'Hindu nationalism' (Banerjee, 2006) – the performance ended with one of the girls coming to the microphone and announcing, to loud approval from the audience: '*kaun kehta hai ki sirf betiyan ghar chorti hain, bete bhi ghar chorte hain, unhe Fauji kehte hain*' (Who says that only daughters leave home (upon getting married), sons too leave home, they are called soldiers). This gave me a cue to ask a neighbour which sport he enjoyed. '*Buddy Kabaddi*' came the unsurprising reply; the favourite team game of the RSS, as it mobilised sports, education, entertainment, information and social service (Jaffrelot, 1999). Each of the above was a political act, providing 'cultural spaces' for various 'bodily practices' of Hindu nationalism, producing 'physiological patriots' (McDonald, 1999, 2003). Next, I asked him about the social composition of the village. He started: 'Brahman, Jat, Kumhar, Chamar, [and] Dhanuk ... *Muslim chor ke chale Gaye*' (the Muslims left). When? '20–30 *saal pehle*' (20–30 years ago). Why? '*Nahin pata, koi panchayat Hui, khud se chale Gaye*' (I do not know. After a village council get-together they left on their own). I was contrasting this 'voluntary' departure of Bhali Anandpur's Muslims with the details of Devru's Muslims, when choreographed gymnastics began, led by a group of teenage boys to the patriotic tunes of '*Chak de India*' (Come on India) and '*Jai Ho*' (Victory).

Labour Minister Nayab Singh Saini arrived on the scene three hours late. He was accompanied by Dev Prakash Bhardwaj, RSS *prant-karyavahak* (state in-charge) for Haryana, Kapil Muni Maharaj of the *Gokarn Teerth* (sect), Seth Manmohan Goyal (a businessman) and Prof Ram Avtar Balmiki (an academic). In other words, the minister's entourage had a Brahmin, a Baba, a Bania and a Balmiki (Dalit). The BJP's electoral engineering of extremes within the Hindu fold (Jha, 2017) was on display. It was a demonstration of 'a particular conception of the Indian nation, in which the Muslims had an unenviable place, the Dalits only symbolically present ... in subordination to the "mainstream, Hindu majority"' (Pandey, 1999). This was also exhibited in the last three items of the cultural programme that Saini and Bhardwaj saw. First was a drama performed by adult men, in which a character announced in frustration, '*Sanskriti ka Sanskrit bana diya, Samajh mein hi nahin Aati*' (We have needlessly complicated 'culture' like 'Sanskrit' [language], one does not understand it anymore), thereby harking back to a simpler, hierarchical world, where everyone knew the culture and their location in it, as opposed to the current, complex world of identity politics. Next, the character of a migrant labourer, from the state of Bihar, was told that if he had come to find work and earn money here, then he had to make sure that his wife and child learnt Haryanvi culture. Both references drew the biggest laughs from the 400-strong audience and I wondered whether a construction of an 'internal other' was a compulsion of the RSS's world view. With a minuscule minority population in the state, who could provide the straw-figure of the outsider inside?

With communalisation confirmed and caste-isation curtailed, the RSS/BJP combine stares at one potential banana skin: agrarian distress. It was brought out in force by a schoolboy, in his poem recital on '*Kisan*' with words like '*Maun khadi Sarkar dekhti, Kisan ke Apmaan ko*' (Silent the government stands watching the insult of farmers). I marvelled at what the minister must be thinking, given that this phraseology has been employed by the present prime minister to lampoon his predecessor? Perhaps to soothe his feathers, next came a girl to recite a poem titled 'Soldier Papa in *Tiranga*'. This performance of 'public rites' and 'patriotic funerals' has pervaded the public sphere since the 1999 India-Pakistan Kargil War (Zins, 2007). The finale was an act of yoga – symbolising the 'somatic nationalism' of militant Hinduism (Alter, 1994) – performed by Salim and Suraj to the song '*Mera Rang de Basanti Chola*' (Mother, colour my tunic saffron), from the 1965 film *Shaheed*. It reflected the RSS's 'conception of exercises … used to inculcate an "instinctive" sense of loyalty to, and love of, the Hindu culture' (McDonald, 1999). Salim was the single instance of Muslim-ness in the air during the day, thereby confirming the near-successful 'digesting [of] the Muslim "other" by Hindu Nationalism', in this part of India (Sharma, 2009).

V

In the RSS's Village Republic, this 'accumulation of spectacle [was] not a collection of images, but a social relation among people' (Harris, 2012). Firstly, the 'political mainstreaming' of the RSS has meant that people have been able to participate in its 'Hindu resurgence', without joining it. Its volunteers are more often teachers, doctors, engineers and civil servants than politicians/ministers. Its 'sleeper cell' nature has meant that electoral office, state power/patronage and social elite notwithstanding, its ability to draw people pre-dates this and remains *sui generis*; more so in the Hindi lands, where it has a linguistic advantage (Harriss, 2015). But, this 'comprehensively mediated way of life' (Debord, 1970) that happens in Haryana or Mewat 'cannot stay' there (Badhwar, 2018). It may not always pay an electoral dividend, but the goalposts of the idea(s) of India have been decisively shifted and, electorally, 'behind the masks of total choice, different forms of the same alienation confront each other' (Debord, 1970).

Hajji Jumma, or Pehlu Khan and Rakbar Khan in Mewat, have no place in this 'quest for an "*ekjatiya rashtra*" (one people nation)' (Pandey, 1999), except as a depoliticised, silent minority: 'strangers and minor subjects', occasional official support as well as social 'tolerance and hospitality' (Kumar, 2013), notwithstanding. From Gujarat to UP, a *Hindu Rashtra* is on the make, 'without any constitutional or legal change'. Some 10% of the former's and 20% of the latter's state populations have little legislative or official representation and even less public articulation. This 'communalism of Indian politics' has to be seen in continuum. Thirty years ago, Romesh Thapar wrote about 'the malignant ruling Congress – pretenders to secularity – and RSS – brazen and crude in their assertions' together transforming 'Hinduistic sentiment into a nationalistic invocation … tearing people apart in the name of phantom unity' (Thapar, 1986). With a change of 'ruling BJP' for Congress, more of the same holds true for today. 'Bigotry' on the latter's watch has been made 'bold' and 'publicly acceptable' under Narendra Modi and the RSS 'is harnessing the returns' (Bal, 2018).

Acknowledgement

I am grateful to Profs. Paul McGarr and Ruth Maxey at Nottingham for the opportunity and the support to first, present, and now, publish, this account. It was put together with Rahul Jayaram, Krithika Ashok and Wajahat Ahmad at Sonipat. Amit Bindal, Prashant Iyengar and Mohsin Raza Khan pushed some of its ideas, while Himanshu Malik provided the occasion to enhance it. Thank you, above all, to Hajji Jumma.

Works cited

Alter, J. (1994). 'Somatic Nationalism: Indian Wrestling and Militant Hinduism'. *Modern Asian Studies*, 28(3), 557–588.
Anderson, P. (2013). *The Indian Ideology*. London: Verso.
Apoorvanand [sic], A. Javed and S. Deshpande (2015). 'Situation Normal, All Fouled Up: Atali Muslims Return Home to an Uneasy Calm'. *Scroll.in*. 17 June. http://scroll.in/article/734750/situation-normal-all-fouled-up-atali-muslims-return-home-to-an-uneasy-calm. Accessed 30 July 2018.
Badhwar, N. (2018). 'What Happens in Mewat Cannot Stay in Mewat'. *The Caravan*. 29 July. https://caravanmagazine.in/crime/what-happens-in-mewat-cannot-stay-in-mewat. Accessed 30 July 2018.
Bal, H. (2018). 'Why Modi's Legacy Will Not Disappear with a Hug and Wink'. *The Caravan*. 24 July. https://caravanmagazine.in/politics/modis-legacy-will-not-disappear-with-hug-wink. Accessed 30 July 2018.
Banerjee, S. (2006). 'Armed Masculinity, Hindu Nationalism and Female Political Participation in India'. *International Feminist Journal of Politics*, 8(1), 62–83.
Bhardwaj, A. (2016). 'Dewarhu: Another Ayodhya in the Making?' *Newslaundry.com*. 20 April. www.newslaundry.com/2016/04/20/dewarhu-another-ayodhya-making/. Accessed 30 July 2018.
Chowdhry, P. (2013). 'Militarised Masculinities: Shaped and Reshaped in Colonial South East Punjab'. *Modern Asian Studies*, 47(3), 713–750.
Copeman, J. (2013). 'The Art of Bleeding: Memory, Martyrdom, and Portraits in Blood'. *Journal of the Royal Anthropological Institute*, 19(1), 149–171.
'The Dadri Lynching: How Events Unfolded' (2015). *The Hindu*. 3 October. www.thehindu.com/specials/in-depth/the-dadri-lynching-how-events-unfolded/article7719414.ece. Accessed 30 July 2018.
Debord, G. (1970). *Society of the Spectacle*. Kalamazoo, MI: Black & Red.
'Fear Grips Muslims in Dewarhu Village in Sonipat, Haryana' (2016). *Sabrang*. 5 April. https://sabrangindia.in/article/fear-grips-muslims-dewarhu-village-sonipat-haryana. Accessed 30 July 2018.
Gould, W. (2004). *Hindu Nationalism and the Language of Politics in Late Colonial India*. Cambridge: Cambridge University Press.
Hansen, T.B. (1999). *The Saffron Wave: Democracy and Hindu Nationalism in Modern India*. Princeton, NJ: Princeton University Press.
Harris, J. (2012). 'Guy Debord Predicted Our Distracted Society'. *The Guardian*. 30 March. www.theguardian.com/commentisfree/2012/mar/30/guy-debord-society-spectacle. Accessed 30 July 2018.
Harriss, J. (2015). 'Hindu Nationalism in Action: The Bharatiya Janata Party and Indian Politics'. *South Asia: Journal of South Asian Studies*, 38(4), 712–718.
Iqbal, M. (1973). *The Sound of the Bell*. Lahore: Shaikh Ghulam Ali.
Jaffrelot, C. (1999). *The Hindu Nationalist Movement and Indian Politics, 1925 to the 1990s: Strategies of Identity-building, Implementation and Mobilisation*. Delhi: Penguin.

Jha, P. (2017). *How the BJP Wins: Inside India's Greatest Election Machine*. Delhi: Juggernaut.

'Jharkhand: Two Muslim Cattle Traders Found Hanging from Tree in Latehar' (2016). *The Indian Express*. 19 March. http://indianexpress.com/article/india/india-news-india/jharkhand-police-probe-cattle-traders-death/. Accessed 30 July 2018.

Jodhka, S. (2002). 'Nation and Village: Images of Rural India in Gandhi, Nehru and Ambedkar'. *Economic and Political Weekly*, 37(32), 3343–3353.

Jones, K. (1976). *Arya Dharm: Hindu Consciousness in 19th-Century Punjab*. Berkeley, CA: University of California Press.

Kaur, R. (2003). *Performative Politics and the Cultures of Hinduism: Public Uses of Religion in Western India*. London: Anthem Press.

Khalidi, O. (2008). 'Hinduising India: Secularism in Practice'. *Third World Quarterly*, 29(8), 1545–1562.

Kudaisya, G. (2006). *Region, Nation, Heartland: Uttar Pradesh in India's Body Politic*. Delhi: Sage.

Kumar, P. (2013). 'Beyond Tolerance and Hospitality: Muslims as Strangers and Minor Subjects in Hindu Nationalist and Indian Nationalist Discourse'. In: E. Weber (ed.) *Living Together: Jacques Derrida's Communities of Violence and Peace*. New York: Fordham University Press, pp. 80–103.

Lal, V. (ed.) (2009). *Political Hinduism*. Delhi: Oxford University Press.

Maclean, K. (2008). *Pilgrimage and Power: The Kumbh Mela in Allahabad*. New York: Oxford University Press, pp. 1765–1954.

McCullough, C.B. (2002). *The Truth of History*. London: Routledge.

McDonald, I. (1999). 'Physiological Patriots?: The Politics of Physical Culture and Hindu Nationalism in India'. *International Review for the Sociology of Sports*, 34(4), 343–358.

McDonald, I. (2003). 'Hindu Nationalism, Cultural Spaces, and Bodily Practices in India'. *American Behavioral Scientist*, 46(11), 1563–1576.

Mukul, A. (2015). *Gita Press and the Making of Hindu India*. Delhi: HarperCollins.

Nair, P. (2009). *Religious Political Parties and Their Welfare Work*. Birmingham University Religions and Development Research Programme, Working Paper 37. www.birmingham.ac.uk/Documents/college-social-sciences/government-society/research/rad/working-papers/wp-37.pdf. Accessed 30 July 2018.

Pandey, G. (1999). 'Can a Muslim Be an Indian?' *Comparative Studies in Society and History*, 41(4), 608–629.

Pandey, P. (2016). 'Jharkhand: Two Cattle Traders Hanged from Tree, Gau Raksha Activist among 5 Held'. *The Indian Express*. 21 March. http://indianexpress.com/article/india/india-news-india/jharkhand-latehar-district-muslim-cattle-traders-hanged-five-arrested-section-144/. Accessed 30 July 2018.

Panikkar, K.N. (1990). 'Introduction'. *Social Scientist*, 18(8/9), 1–3.

Patwardhan, A. (dir.) (1992). *In the Name of God* (*Ram Ke Naam*) (http://patwardhan.com/wp/?page_id=178).

Purushotham, S. (2015). 'Internal Violence: The "Police Action" in Hyderabad'. *Comparative Studies in Society and History*, 57(2), 435–466.

Ramaswamy, S. (2008). 'Maps, Mothers/Goddesses, and Martyrdom in Modern India'. *The Journal of Asian Studies*, 67(3), 819–853.

Raychaudhuri, D. (2017). 'The Synthesis: Acceptance of the Political Hindu'. *Mainstream Weekly*. 13 May. www.mainstreamweekly.net/article7164.html. Accessed 30 July 2018.

Robinson, A. (2011). 'In Theory: Bakhtin: Dialogism, Polyphony and Heteroglossia'. *Ceasefire*. 29 July. https://ceasefiremagazine.co.uk/in-theory-bakhtin-1/. Accessed 30 July 2018.

Sharma, J. (2009). 'Digesting the "Other": Hindu Nationalism and the Muslims in India'. In: V. Lal (ed.) *Political Hinduism*. Delhi: Oxford University Press, pp. 150–172.

Stoler, A. (2010). 'Archival Dis-Ease: Thinking through Colonial Ontologies'. *Communication and Critical/Cultural Studies*, 7(2), 215–219.

Thapar, R. (1986). *These Troubled Times* ... Bombay: Popular Prakashan.

Vachani, L. (dir.) (1993). *The Boy in the Branch* (A Wide Eye Film production for "South," Channel Four Television, UK; http://www.lalitvachani.com/film05.html), (https://www.imdb.com/title/tt7814260/plotsummary?ref_=tt_ov_pl).

Van der Veer, P. (1994). *Religious Nationalism: Hindus and Muslims in India*. Berkeley, CA: University of California Press.

Weber, E. (ed.) (2013) *Living Together: Jacques Derrida's Communities of Violence and Peace*. New York: Fordham University Press.

Yadav, A. (2015). 'Fifty Kilometres from Delhi, Hundreds of Muslims Have Become Refugees Overnight'. *Scroll.in*. 29 May. http://scroll.in/article/730652/fifty-kilometres-from-delhi-hundreds-of-muslims-have-become-refugees-overnight. Accessed 30 July 2018.

Zins, M. (2007). 'Public Rites and Patriotic Funerals: The Heroes and the Martyrs of the 1999 Indo-Pakistan Kargil War'. *India Review*, 6(1), 25–45.

4 Cartooning politics

Reading the *Daily Mail, Dawn* and *Hindustan Times*

Nassif Muhammed Ali

Cartoons' essential nature of being subjective rather than objective makes them more interesting for an historian; for it makes it easier to grasp the various perspectives that existed in a society by reading cartoons of a particular period of time in history. One way in which this can be achieved is by reading cartoons from different sources discussing the same set of events (Douglas, 2009, 12). As a medium that targets incongruities by being opinionated and strident, newspaper cartoons can, therefore, provide fresh perspectives on political discourses. It is by leaning on such an assumption that this study steps forward, and attempts to untangle underlying attitudes in political scenarios as reflected in cartoons dealing with the transfer of power in India in the late 1940s. This becomes crucial when we note that the media in general, and cartoons in particular, have a key role in influencing the public (Sani et al., 2012). According to Kemnitz (1973), the political cartoon 'can match any other media for invective and is an excellent method for disseminating highly emotional attitudes'; it is also used widely as 'a weapon of propaganda' (84).

The subjective views expressed by political cartoons, therefore, provide us with a plethora of perspectives with which to look at the past – perspectives that would be missing in a factual and rational report or document. In the particular context of this chapter, one gets to see how each of the hostile camps concerned with Indian independence viewed each other and, more important, wanted to depict the other to their own readerships. It is intriguing, therefore, to observe how cartoons were used to depict disagreements and differences in arguments in an Indian political scenario rife with conflicting interests. What do these depictions tell us about the cartoonists? How do these cartoons enrich existing historical narratives? What kind of response did they generate from the characters within the frame and without? And, most important, how do these engagements differ from current political scenarios? These are the questions that this chapter addresses by reading cartoons from three different British and Indian newspapers – the *Daily Mail, Dawn* and the *Hindustan Times* – during the last years of colonial rule in India. The *Daily Mail* was, as it proclaimed itself, the newspaper that stood for King and Empire (Bryant, 2009, 16–19). *Dawn*, on the other hand, was established by Mohamed Ali Jinnah, the founder of the Muslim League. It represented the Muslim League in public in the same way that the *Hindustan Times* reflected opinion from within the Indian National Congress (Tanwar, 2006, 14–15).

The Second World War forced a weakened British government to negotiate with the major political parties in India in an effort to garner their support in the war. Stafford Cripps, a member of the British War Cabinet, arrived in India on a mission in 1942 to woo nationalist leaders (Sarkar, 1989, 385). The failure of Cripps's mission led the Congress to initiate the Quit India protest movement (Sarkar, 1989, 388–404). The British Indian government arrested the top leaders of the Congress before protests commenced, which infuriated Indian opinion and resulted in widespread opposition and violence. In 1946, following the war, a three-member delegation, comprising the First Lord of the Admiralty, A.V. Alexander, the Secretary of State for India, Pethick Lawrence, and Cripps was sent to India. They arrived at a point when communal violence and famines were threatening to tear Indian society apart. Subsequent discussions focused on forming an Indian government for an interim period by establishing a coalition between the Indian National Congress and the Muslim League. This, it was hoped, would undertake decisive administrative measures as well as oversee a smooth transfer of power. When this attempt failed, the viceroy invited Congress to form a government without the League. On 2 September 1946, Congress inaugurated an interim government. Attempts at power sharing did continue and, at a later stage, the Muslim League joined the interim government's ranks. The friction between political parties was, however, deep and widened into a discord between the two dominant religious communities in the subcontinent, ending in partition accompanied by communal bloodshed (Wolpert, 2006, 9–11).

Ahmed, *Dawn* and Azad

Enver Ahmed, who began his career as a cartoonist at the *Pioneer*, subsequently moved on to *Dawn* and, from there, eventually, to the *Hindustan Times*. To his credit, Ahmed's work as a cartoonist, despite the febrile political environment in which he operated, was influenced and characterised by biting critique and sharp satire. Before his involvement with the Congress, Abul Kalam Azad was an active member of the League and a favourite subject for Ahmed. Azad's 'Pan-Islamist' views during this phase were considered dangerous by the British (Hasan, 2004, 41). Thus, before 1920, his focus was predominantly on the Muslim community and the need to develop its collective identity (Datta, 1990, 107). However, during the Khilafat and Non-cooperation movement, he realised that co-operation between Hindus and Muslims was possible. He justified this by citing examples of the Prophet Muhammed, who had formed alliances with non-Muslims (Hasan, 55). Azad grew distant from the League as a consequence of his increasing closeness to Gandhi, Congress and nationalist politics.

It was during his second tenure as the Congress president, beginning in 1940, that the Muslim League raised the call for a separate Muslim nation. Azad's opposition to this move made him a thorn in the flesh of the League. This manifested in open verbal attacks as well as personal criticism of Azad.

Cartooning politics 63

Such expressions of resentment were frequent in the cartoons published in *Dawn*, a League mouthpiece. A selection of such cartoons are critically analysed in the text that follows.

The first cartoon examined dates from 21 March 1946, and appeared against the background of British Prime Minister Clement Attlee's statement discounting the possibility that a minority group in India could veto the will of the majority (Mahajan, 2000, 147; see Figure 4.1). It shows a wall, on which is written 'Pakistan' in upper case and with a halo around it – this being the 'indelible' writing mentioned in the title. Prominent Congress leaders and former presidents of the party, Mohandas Karamchand Gandhi, Jawaharlal Nehru and Vallabhai Patel, are depicted. Nehru is trying to erase the text using a cloth, Gandhi sits with a furnace of sorts, cooking up 'the Attlee minorities Exterminator', and spraying it at the writing on the wall. Meanwhile, Patel is holding an axe tagged 'civil war', and aiming to break the wall down. Thus, while Nehru is trying to erase the idea of Pakistan, Gandhi's action implies Congress's willingness to join hands with the British for that purpose. Patel is shown as more militant, wielding the axe of civil war. What is important here is how Azad is depicted. Lying down on all fours, he is a stool for Nehru to stand on; thereby implying that Congress was exploiting a compliant Azad.

In a second cartoon, Azad is depicted as a horse tied to a hackney carriage ridden by Gandhi, pictured as a 'Bikri Walla', who 'buys and sells almost anything', a malnourished horse at that (see Figure 4.2). The title, 'Not yet Master, we still need each other, is a response to the quote by Jinnah shown in the background,

Figure 4.1 Indelible Writing on the Wall. Cartoon by Enver Ahmed (Courtesy: *Dawn*, 21 March 1946).

Figure 4.2 Not Yet master, We Still Need Each Other. Cartoon by Enver Ahmed (Courtesy: *Dawn*, March 1946).

which reads 'Congress hackney should be pensioned off'. The implication is that Congress had bought Azad and would not think much of selling him off if need be – as it 'buys and sells almost anything'. It also asserts the notion that Azad was no less than the slave of Congress leaders, a theme in common with the previous cartoon.

A further cartoon published on 4 April 1946, entitled *Loaves and Fishes*, depicts the dining room of the Indian Cabinet of 1937 (see Figure 4.3). The only person eating, however, is Pandit Pant, who was then the financial, as well as the home minister, of the United Provinces. While his plate is overloaded, the rest of the ministers only have morsels on their plates. This indicates the lack of funds ministries were receiving. Behind Pandit Pant stands Azad, who is depicted as a 'Wine Waiter' – with 'Traitor's port' and 'Quisling Sherry' on his menu. Quisling, traitor and collaborator were adjectives used by the Muslim League and *Dawn* to describe Azad. The cartoon, therefore, implies that as a quisling, the best things he can offer are Traitor's port and Quisling Sherry. Or, to put it in other words, what better could Azad offer the Congress and its ministry than his role as a 'traitor' to his co-religionists?

The biggest insult contained in these cartoons comes on 4 May 1946, in a work titled 'Congress Retrievers' (see Figure 4.4). This cartoon shows the entire delegation at the Shimla talks addressing the transfer of power – which includes Jinnah and Liaqat Ali Khan on the League side, and Nehru and Patel on the Congress side, along with the three British cabinet mission representatives.

Figure 4.3 Loaves and Fishes. Cartoon by Enver Ahmed (Courtesy: *Dawn*, 4 April 1946).

Figure 4.4 Congress Retrievers. Cartoon by Enver Ahmed (Courtesy: *Dawn*, 4 May 1946).

The Muslim League was opposed to the idea of recognising any non-League Muslims as part of independence negotiations, whether it was regarding an interim government or the terms of self-rule and partition, in an attempt to establish the League as the sole representatives of Muslims in India. This was unacceptable to the Congress, as they claimed to represent all sections of Indian society (Mahajan, 2000, 299). Thus, it was a provocation as far as the League was concerned, when Congress included Azad and Khan Abdul Ghaffar Khan – a Congress leader from the North-West Frontier Province and a Muslim – in their delegation to Simla (Moon, 1973, 264).

There are two dogs hidden behind Nehru's and Patel's legs in the first frame of the cartoon. The mission, in the very first frame, tries to throw away the bone of deadlock, which is defined as the Congress claims of Muslim representation. This, however, sets the two dogs off and they bring the bone back. The dogs are none other than Azad and Khan Abdul Ghaffar Khan. The implication, as the accompanying text suggests, is that by an ill-judged selection of members for the deliberations, Congress was threatening to thwart the discussions.

The argument this essay advances is that cartoons offer perspectives on history that enhance viewpoints reproduced in more traditional textual sources. It therefore becomes important to note how the cartoons in *Dawn* pictured Abul Kalam Azad and bestowed on him the titles of 'Congress Showboy', 'Quisling' and 'Traitor'. From depicting him as Gandhi's horse, it goes on to show him as the Congress's dog.

Illingworth, the *Daily Mail* and Indian politics

Leslie Gilbert Illingworth had worked as an illustrator for 13 years before he joined the *Daily Mail*. When the *Daily Mail* advertised for a political cartoonist, Illingworth saw it as the chance to serve his country in the best way he knew how. However, he also believed that a cartoonist must have a pragmatic approach to his work and thought of himself as 'very venal'. 'I knew which side of my bread was buttered', he would say later (Bryant, 2009, 16). During the Second World War, he drew no less than 1,018 cartoons (Bryant, 2009, 23). These cartoons reached the readers through a newspaper, the *Daily Mail*, that was 'sympathetic to the fighting man' and had a strong hold in the British market (Bryant, 2009, 19). Illingworth's cartoons were sufficiently influential to be used by the British government propaganda service, the Ministry of Information.

One notable Illingworth cartoon examined threats looming in the Indian subcontinent. Entitled 'Three Innocents in the jungle of India/Pakistan', it sympathises with the members of the British cabinet mission who are 'stranded' in the jungle of India, where awaiting them is a Congress elephant, a Muslim League snake, and a ferocious tiger, symbolising famine. The cartoon conveys the message that India is a dangerous jungle inhabited by dangerous troublemakers such as Congress and the League, where apparently famine is a problem over which the British bear no responsibility. A second cartoon, published on 14 May 1946, depicted the struggle for power between Indian leaders. Here a woman – symbolising India – is scared by the approach of a tiger and a jackal, which are tagged as civil war and famine respectively. The 'men' in the cartoon are Gandhi, Jinnah and Cripps, who are all safely sitting atop a tree. The first two are locked in conflict over the new constitution while 'India' is in a deep predicament, vulnerable to attacks from wild animals. It is a British critique of Indian leaders, who, according to the cartoonist, have left Indian people vulnerable to threats while they themselves selfishly scramble for power.

Both cartoons directly address famine as an important element in Indian politics, personified in the first instance as a ferocious tiger and in the second as a jackal. However, there is no mention of the cause of famine, or with whom responsibility for it lies. The fact that famine is associated with Congress and the League in the first cartoon implies that it is Indian parties that are responsible for the situation. However, it was in the provinces 'best administered' by the colonial government that the famine struck harder, as the viceroy himself acknowledged (Moon, 1973, 202). It appears that the cartoonist chose to conveniently overlook this reality.

After several rounds of fruitless talks and conciliatory noises between the Congress and the Muslim League, the Congress established sole control of an interim government in 1946. This breakdown was due to demands made by the League, which included parity of Muslim and Hindu members in the interim government, a condition that Congress found unacceptable. The League subsequently passed a resolution stating that it was 'Congress intransigence' and a breach of trust by the British government that led to a breakdown in relations (Mansergh and Moon, 1981, 135–139). The League also resolved to take direct action to achieve its goal of a separate Muslim state, Pakistan, and called on its followers to be ready for any kind of sacrifice towards this end (Mansergh and Moon, 1981, 239–240). In response, the viceroy invited Nehru to form an interim government (Mansergh and Moon, 1981, 188), and, on 2 September 1946, it came into power (Sarkar, 1989, 431).

The last months of 1946 found the subcontinent falling into the grasp of riots and massacres. Bengal, Punjab, United Provinces, and Bihar were affected by violence (Sarkar, 1989, 432–433). On 17 December, a cartoon was published in the *Daily Mail* with the caption, 'But can they?' It shows an open cage out of which a ferocious tiger – Civil War – emerges. Nehru is depicted opening the cage from above, out of cowardice. Lying at a safe distance, Nehru asks the British to leave India and claims that the country can do without them. Here, the cartoonist is criticising the Congress leadership, accusing them of being at least partly responsible for causing violence and civil war, and suggesting that they are incapable of facing up to its consequences, or to putting an end to it. A soldier, representing the British, places himself valiantly between the beast and a vulnerable lady (embodying the Indian people) who is carrying a baby. The question raised by the caption, therefore, could be summarised as: what could the Indian leaders do without the help of courageous and able British officers?

An additional cartoon, published on 28 August, was captioned 'Race Hatred'. It presents a woman named 'the Minorities', on her knees, crying for help.

A ghastly looking man in typical North Indian attire, label 'Race Hatred', grabs her and rushes towards what seems to be the sanctuary of a British official. The British official is seen exiting his office, leaving a cigarette to burn out. The reason for his departure seems to be a letter on a table that reads, 'Renunciation of British Sovereignty'. The use of the term 'race', however, is problematic considering the fact that the riots were communal, not racial in their nature. Illingworth was not the first to use the term 'race' to denote conflicts between communities in India. As early as January 1946, in a speech following League victories in provincial elections, Vallabhbhai Patel stated, 'many races have come and settled here. Some are claiming to be a separate nation and are demanding partition of India' (Sarkar and Bhatacharya, 2008, 274). Patel was not alone in thinking along such lines. In April 1946, addressing the Muslim League Legislators' Council, Suhrawardy had proclaimed that 'The Muslims wanted to be the ruling race in this sub-continent' (Sarkar and Bhatacharya, 2008, 405). A further point to note is the cartoon's notion of a void that is left behind by the British. It is suggestive that Indian leaders, who have already been tagged ignorant, cowardly and idle, are inept as well. Examining Illingworth's cartoons in this way also underlines a willingness to marginalise and ignore the existence of national movements of any sort. The predominant narrative is of the valiant British saving India from troubles posed by nationalist leaders and broader Indian society.

Illingworth's cartoons convey significant meaning and a powerful political subtext. The depiction of India, its society, social situation, and its political parties evidences a connective. Many of these cartoons have women as characters. Frightened and vulnerable, they are tagged as India, its people or its minority communities. The use of gender stereotypes is a tried and tested technique in political cartoons. Wickham, in her study of cartoons on German unification, has explained the depiction of women and the stereotypes and sexism that cartoonists employed (Wickham, 1998, 156). It is evident that a similar pattern was followed in Illingworth's cartoons. It must also be noted that in one cartoon a British soldier valiantly stands in front of a tiger to save India and it is the same soldier who makes a point in another cartoon with his absence. The British are characterised in Illingworth's cartoons as innocent men, valiant and courageous soldiers, mediators and saviours forced out of office.

Illingworth's use of animal imagery is also noteworthy. Tropical animals, elephants, and tigers appear. While it is India and the Indian National Congress that are depicted as elephants, the tiger is used to depict the Japanese army that was then knocking at the North-East gates of India during the Second World War, as well as famine and civil war. Famine is depicted in another situation as a hungry jackal. On the other hand, the Muslim League appears in a cartoon as a snake. The implication links the League to the wily and cunning nature of snakes. As to the background setting, Illingworth employs a wild jungle, a riot scene, or fire and rising smoke in most cases, implying an attribution of a wild and uncivilised nature to Indian society.

Underlying these depictions is an attempt to look down on India and its society as weak, vulnerable and afraid of internal threats like famine, civil war and communal riots (while at the same time being responsible for them all), and a self-proclamation of the British as a saviour. Repeated use of the image of the elephant symbolises stubbornness – or another way of reading the persistent waves of national resistance to British rule. The elephant, it must be remembered is an animal, which in spite of its massive strength and size, can be tamed by human beings. This lays bare the British outlook on Indian society. Edward Said has referenced the practice of designating in one's mind a familiar space as 'ours', and an unfamiliar space beyond 'ours' as 'theirs', as entirely arbitrary. Said goes on to say that for the West, 'Asia is defeated and distant', and a 'dangerous space beyond familiar boundaries' (Said 1978, 54–57). This is reflected in Illingworth's work, though when taking into consideration his audience, the daily newspaper that he worked for and the sources of news that he had access to, this is of little surprise.

Shankar and the *Quaid*

Shankar's cartoons prior to the independence of India have been regarded as an integral part of the *Hindustan Times*, a newspaper aligned with Congress (Tanwar, 2006, 60–87). Even more significant, Shankar's cartoons had an important role to play in India's movement for independence (Sudheernath, 2012, 41). The sheer craft of his cartoons, their satire and the humour delivered underline the importance of analysing cartoons as a medium for social and political agency. The counterpoint to Ahmed's 'Azad' was Shankar's 'Jinnah', along with representations of his aide, Liaqat Ali Khan. This is not very surprising, considering how Jinnah dominated the Muslim League. 'We stand for one leader, one voice, one aim' was how Suhrawardy, a League leader from Bengal, put it (Sarkar and Bhatacharya, 2008, 405).

The first Jinnah cartoon considered is undated (see Figure 4.5). It was cited in the book *Tragedy of Jinnah*, published in 1941. The cartoon, titled 'Blitzkrieg', focuses on Jinnah as an ambitious expansionist, and Liaqat Ali Khan as his draughtsman. Blitzkrieg denotes a sudden military charge and attack, aimed at securing a quick victory. Jinnah is giving instructions on how to mark the map of the Indian subcontinent. Shankar has divided the frame into six. In the first frame, Jinnah rejects Liaqat's drawing that demarcates what seem to be Punjab on the west and Bengal in the east. In the next frame, Liaqat adds Hyderabad, only to be rejected by Jinnah yet again. Liaqat then darkens the North-West Frontier Province and Sindh in the west, and much of the United Provinces, Bihar and Orissa, only for Jinnah to show disinterest. A demarcation of almost the whole subcontinent, excepting a little of Gujarat and Maharashtra, also fail to impress Jinnah, who exclaims 'not enough'. Subsequently, Jinnah is upset by the fact that the tip of South India has been excluded. Once that too is filled in on the map, and the whole subcontinent, including Ceylon, is labelled as Pakistan, the boss and his draughtsman are finally happy and satisfied. The cartoonist is ridiculing Muslim League politics and in the process critiquing Jinnah's demands in general as unreasonable, illogical and whimsical. It pictures Liaqat Ali Khan as an

70 *Nassif Muhammed Ali*

Figure 4.5 Blitzkrieg. Cartoon by Shankar, *Hindustan Times* (Courtesy: *Tragedy of Jinnah*).

obedient follower of the Quaid-e-Azam. This cartoon is interesting in that it is not presented as a single frame, which is Shankar's style. He has split the frame down into six cells, giving the whole cartoon the effect of a comic strip.

On 20 March 1946, slightly before the arrival of the British cabinet mission in India, the *Hindustan Times* published a cartoon titled 'Congrophobia' (see Figure 4.6). The similar ring that the word 'Congrophobia' has with 'claustrophobia' is not coincidental. Freud defines such instances where two words are combined by overlapping them as 'condensation accompanied by the formation of a substitute' which according to him is one important technique of mimicry (Freud, 1971, 16–20). The cartoon shows Jinnah in his traditional attire standing in the midst of an unruly crowd that comprises men, women and youth – most of them in Congress-caps, and a few wearing masks, suggesting that they may be criminals. Visibly shaken and taken aback by the crowd, Jinnah has just had the fright of his life. The implication is, as reinforced by text reproduced below the cartoon, Jinnah's anxiety about the kind of atmosphere in which the cabinet mission discussions were about to take place. The crowd is pictured beyond a wave of light that appears around the main character's image, denoting its presence in Jinnah's imagination. The suggestion being that his anxiety was misplaced.

A further Shankar cartoon published on 2 April offered the cartoonist's view of the Indian princes' attempts to bring together the Congress and the Muslim League (see Figure 4.7). The princes and Indian political leaders are pictured as

Figure 4.6 Congrophobia. Cartoon by Shankar (Courtesy: *The Hindustan Times*, 20 March 1946).

Figure 4.7 Nothing Doing. Cartoon by Shankar (Courtesy: *The Hindustan Times*, 2 April 1946).

72 *Nassif Muhammed Ali*

cupids trying to make the couple fall for each other. The 'couple' in question are, however, Abul Kalam Azad and 'lady' Jinnah. Azad has clearly succumbed to the first arrow to hit him and is sitting on the ground, surrendering to love. However, the lady, visibly obstinate and arrogant, as the facial expression tells us, holds her ground and remains still. The arrows have bent in front of her obstinacy. The implication is that Congress is amiable and amenable when it comes to reconciliation, while the Muslim League is obstinate and arrogant. The personification of the obstinate Jinnah as a woman, as the pejorative gender stereotypes that it reinforces, should be noted here.

A further cartoon, 'The Parity Business', published on 8 June, is the first to confront the topic of 'Parity' or political power sharing (see Figure 4.8). As the possibility of an interim coalition government at the national level became clearer, Jinnah demanded parity with his counterparts in Congress in terms of the number of ministers that each party controlled. Logically, this was absurd, as it meant that two parties, that represented starkly different sizes of populations, would receive the same number of representatives in government. Jinnah claimed that he had secured the viceroy's agreement to a power sharing formula of 5:5:2 (five ministers for Congress, five for the League and one each for Sikhs and Christians) when they had met at Simla. He elaborated that it was on the basis of this formula that he persuaded the Muslim League Working Committee to agree to join the government. Jinnah alleged that there was a sinister attempt on the part of the Congress media to sabotage this formula, and made it clear that any diversion from it would not be acceptable to the League, and would lead them to reject the invitation to join the government. He also warned that if Congress made any attempt to

Figure 4.8 The Parity Business. Cartoon by Shankar (Courtesy: *The Hindustan Times*, 8 June 1946).

include a Muslim in their Cabinet quota, it would offend the League (Mansergh and Moon, 1981, 841–842). The cartoonist here attempts to depict the absurdity of these demands by drawing a set of scales, with Jinnah – as a child – sitting on the one side, while the lady Congress and her children sit on the other. The scales, however, hang evenly in spite of this variation in weight, much to the elation of Jinnah and to the disappointment of the lady and her children. Jinnah's depiction as the prankish infant is no coincidence: it formed an overt attempt to present his demands as childish and ill-conceived.

Before considering Shankar's cartoons as a whole, it is worthwhile analysing Shankar's Jinnah more closely. Jinnah may be the character that Shankar covered most in his cartoons penned before independence. Shankar's 'Jinnah' is lean. He is depicted as a child or a short man in comparison to the Congress leaders – the former to denote the childishness of Jinnah's whims, and the latter to underline how politically regressive he was in comparison with Congress leaders. Clad mostly in either a traditional *kurta-pajama* or a Western suit of black, 'Jinnah' sports a monocle with a long string that hangs down like a tag. Add to this the slick combed hair and there is no missing the Quaid, as far as the reader is concerned. It had all the poise of the *League Fuehrer*, as the *Hindustan Times* labelled Jinnah (Sarkar and Bhattacharya, 2008, 405–406). It was so sharp and critical that Gandhi himself criticised Shankar, saying that he was crossing the limits of propriety when lampooning Jinnah (Khanduri, 2014, 102).

Unlike Ahmed, his counterpart in Pakistan, Shankar found a congenial home for his work. His first break in the *Hindustan Times* had been secured through lauding Congress and lampooning the British. He was given full freedom by the newspaper's board. One has to assume that this advantage helped Shankar's reputation, and his subsequent capacity for being equated with the very notion of political cartoons and satire in India. Likewise, the twists and turns and political difficulties Ahmed encountered in his career may have pushed him into obscurity.

Looking at the same sequence of events, or the same socio-political landscape through the medium of cartoons derived from different sources, is instructive. It warrants a comparative reading of cartoonists and their techniques. One parameter for comparing cartoons lies in the detail with which they are drawn. While Ahmed and Illingworth are keen on the intricacies of characters, Shankar's cartoons and characters are comparatively simple. Similarly, as far as background context is concerned, Illingworth and Ahmed provide detailed backdrops for their work. Here, the politics is played out as much in the background as in the foreground of cartoons. In Illingworth's cartoons on India, the action usually focuses on the wilderness of a jungle, while in Ahmed's cartoons, it is the urban spaces of streets, roads and walls that feature. One could easily see that while the former found the political scenario in India as something wild and uncivilised, the latter accords an urban and more contemporary character to it. Shankar on the other hand invariably does not work up a detailed background. His focus is on the political actors. In fact, these elements place Shankar's works closer to that of the British cartoonist, David Low. That Shankar had gone to London and trained with Low for some time underscores this connection (Sudheernath, 2012, 25).

Characterisation and personification form another plane for comparison. Here it must be noted that Shankar's cartoons feature human subjects. The point being that personification of animals, a widely used technique by cartoonists including Ahmed, Illingworth, and even Low (with whom Shankar shares some ideas), is absent in Shankar's works. The animals Ahmed and Illingworth use, and the way in which they do so, are important. The animals Ahmed uses in his cartoons are domesticated – typically horses, donkeys and dogs; while Illingworth's animals include tigers, elephants, wolves and snakes. This makes sense when placed within the context of the political backgrounds that these cartoonists emphasised in their work. Domesticated animals fit smoothly into the urban spaces favoured by Ahmed, whereas wild and ferocious animals of the tropics are a good fit for the jungles depicted in Illingworth's cartoons.

Sukeshi Kamra has noted the power of print culture as a social mediator in the subcontinent, and how this is reflected in the attention that political leaders pay to newspaper coverage, and in the responses that coverage draws from readers, most obviously in letters to editors (2002, 38). A common belief amongst Indian political leaders of the agency exercised by the press has manifested in attempts at controlling media content and turning it to their advantage. Likewise, negative press coverage invariably produces howls of complaint from political parties and charges of bias and misrepresentation (Kamra, 2002, 38–39). Seventy years after India's independence, and with a culture of democratic governance well established, the reaction towards cartoons in the subcontinent is now more politically incendiary than ever. In the recent past, India's citizens have been arrested not just for producing and publishing cartoons, but for simply sharing them with others. In this context, the cartoonist, E.P. Unny, in an interview with Chitra Padmanabhan (2015), reflected that 'under the influence of an emerging brand of mainstream politics, social attitudes are hardening into extreme positions'. Further, Unny added that, 'the first casualty in the media in such a circumstance is the day's cartoon – because as a sharply expressed opinion, it is also one-sided' (Padmanabhan, 2015). The capacity of cartoons to provide a unique window on the evolution of the Indian state, and their importance as a wider barometer of the nation's political health, remains as relevant now as it was at the birth of the Indian Republic, some seven decades ago.

Works cited

Bryant, M. (2009). *Illingworth's War in Cartoons: One Hundred of His Greatest Drawings 1939–1945*. London: Grub Street.

Burke, J. 'Indian Cartoonist Aseem Trivedi Jailed after Arrest on Sedition Charges'. *The Guardian*. 10 September. www.theguardian.com/world/2012/sep/10/indian-cartoonist-jailed-sedition. Accessed 5 January 2019.

Chandra, K. (1941). *Tragedy of Jinnah*. Lahore: Sharma.

Datta, V.N. (1990). *Maulana Azad*. New Delhi: Manohar.

Douglas, R. (2009). 'Cartoons and the Historian'. *Historian*, 102, 12.

Freud, S. (1971). *Jokes and Their Relation to the Unconscious*. Harmondsworth: Penguin.

Hasan, M. (2004). *Islam, Pluralism, Nationhood*. New Delhi: Niyogi Books.
Illingworth, L.G. (1946–1947). *Daily Mail*. British Cartoon Archive, University of Kent.
Kamra, S. (2002). *Bearing Witness: Partition, Independence, End of Raj*. Calgary, Canada: University of Calgary Press.
Kemnitz, T.M. (1973). 'The Cartoon as a Historical Source'. *The Journal of Interdisciplinary History*, 4(1), 81–93.
Khanduri, R.G. (2014). *Caricaturing Culture in India: Cartoons and History in the Modern World*. Cambridge: Cambridge University Press.
Mahajan, S. (2000). *Independence and Partition: The Erosion of Colonial Power in India*. New Delhi: Sage.
Mansergh, N. and Moon, P. (1981). *Constitutional Relations between Britain and India; the Transfer of Power, 1942–7: The Mountbatten Viceroyalty: Formulation of a Plan, 22 March–30 May 1947* (Vol. 10). London: HM Stationery Office.
Moon, P. (1973). *Wavell: The Viceroy's Journal*. London: Oxford University Press.
Padmanabhan, C. (2015). 'The Growing Shrillness of Politics is a Problem for the Cartoonist'. *The Wire*. 8 December. https://thewire.in/media/the-growing-shrillness-of-politics-is-a-problem-for-the-cartoonist. Accessed 5 January 2019.
Said, E. (1978). *Orientalism: Western Representations of the Orient*. New York: Pantheon.
Sani, I., Abdullah, M.H., Abdullah, F.S. and Ali, A.M. (2012). 'Political Cartoon as a Vehicle of Setting Social Agenda: The Newspaper Example'. *Asian Social Science*, 8(6), 156–164.
Sarkar, S. (1989). *Modern India 1885–1947*. Basingstoke: Palgrave Macmillan.
Sarkar, S. and Bhattacharya, S. (eds.) (2008). *Towards Freedom: Documents on the Movement for Independence in India, 1946, Part 1*. New Delhi: Oxford University Press.
Sudheernath (2012). *Sankar: Varayude Punarvaayana (Sankar: Rereading the Lines)*. Priyadarsini Publications.
Tanwar, R. (2006). *Reporting the Partition of Punjab, 1947: Press, Public, and Other Opinions*. New Delhi: Manohar.
Wickham, B.C. (1998). 'Gender in Cartoons of German Unification'. *Journal of Women's History*, 10(1), 127–156.
Wolpert, S. (2006). *Shameful Flight: The Last Years of the British Empire in India*. New York: Oxford University Press.

Part II
Aesthetic responses to Indian modernity

5 The experience of the Left cultural movement in India: 1942 to the present

Arjun Ghosh

The contrast could not have been greater. In the general elections for the lower house of the Indian parliament – the Lok Sabha or the 'house of the people' – in 2004, the Left parties[1] won 61 seats: their highest ever tally. However, in the Lok Sabha elections held in 2014, the Left parties managed to secure only ten seats: the lowest ever. By 2018 the Left also lost control of its governments in West Bengal and Tripura.[2] Both electorally and politically, the Left in India finds itself in a position of immense challenge today. Militant Left parties, like the Communist Party of India (Maoist) or CPI, that have abjured participation in elections in what they term to be a 'bourgeois democracy', have also found it to be a difficult period. The Maoists, whose stated objective is to overthrow the government by creating 'liberated zones', have also registered a drastic decline in the districts under their influence. However, the conditions of the poor in India remain severe. As the number of Indians among the richest in the world rises, India's measure in the human development index has remained abysmally low. This exponential rise in disparities perpetuates a condition that remains ripe for the politics of the Left.

The Left in India was faced with a similar challenge many decades earlier during the Second World War (WWII). At the beginning of WWII, the undivided CPI – an organisation banned by the British colonial administration – followed the directive of the Communist International and opposed the British war effort terming the war to be one fuelled by 'inter-imperialist' rivalry. When the CPI declared its support for the British war effort after June 1941, the colonial government responded by lifting its ban on the party. This enabled the CPI to function with greater openness and led to a rise in its own membership and that of allied trade unions and organisations. The membership of the CPI rose drastically – 4,000 in 1942; 15,000 in May 1943; 53,000 in mid-1946; and over 100,000 by February 1948 (Sarkar, 1983, 413). However, the CPI's opposition to the Quit India movement and the Indian National Army (INA) caused it to be alienated from large sections of the people, particularly in Bengal.

In 1942–1943 the war, an indifferent colonial administration, and an apathetic Bengali middle class caused a man-made famine in Bengal that saw large-scale death and destitution among the peasantry. The CPI and its allied organisations put together a relief effort which perhaps overreached its organisational capacity. The massive effort undertaken by the Communists earned them enormous public support, especially among intellectuals and young people. Aiding this effort were the cultural squads of the Indian People's Theatre Association (IPTA) and the play *Nabanna* (*The New Harvest*, 1944) by Bijon Bhattacharya, which was performed to middle-class audiences in Calcutta and later to audiences across Bengal (Ghosh, 2018). The Bombay branch of the IPTA staged the dance drama *Bhookha Hai Bangal* (*Voice of Bengal*, 1944), choreographed by Shanti Bardhan with its music composed by Abani Dasgupta. This dance drama, along with other pieces put together by the Central Squad of the IPTA, was used to campaign for famine relief efforts across India (Damodaran, 2017, 100). *Nabanna* was adapted into a full-length feature film in Hindi – *Dharti ke Laal* (*Children of the Earth*, 1946) – directed by Khwaja Ahmed Abbas (Rahim, 1969). Not only did these and other pieces succeed in generating resources for the relief effort towards the victims of the Bengal famine, they also attracted a cross-section of artists and intellectuals towards the Communists. Most important, as the membership figures of the CPI stated earlier show, the Communists were able to turn isolation in the national political landscape into a degree of relevance. I would argue that along with the activism of the trade unions and youth organisations, the cultural organisations allied with the CPI – the IPTA in particular – played a crucial role in explaining the position of the Communists to the people and mobilising support towards their policies. However, the impact of the making and performance of *Nabanna* and other presentations by the IPTA stretched far beyond the immediate objectives of famine relief and consolidating the support base of the CPI. The experiences of this period substantially impacted the trajectory of the development of arts and culture in post-independence India.

In this chapter I will trace a brief history of the influence of the Left theatre and cultural movement from the period just prior to independence in 1947 to the present. The trajectory of the Left theatre and cultural movement is closely related to that of the political organisations that constitute the Left in India. In fact, it may be argued that for the Left, cultural and artistic activities play the role of pathfinder and beacon that enables the population to imagine a world view different from the existing one. While the trade unions and other organisations do engage oppressed people in struggles that form a learning experience for them, teaching them to analyse their condition of oppression, identify their oppressor and strategise on ameliorating their condition, it is the artistic and cultural movement that is able to open before them a newer horizon of a world that could be different from the current oppressive one. A study of the rise and fall of the Left movement in India will show that the Left has been able to arise from moments of crisis only through immersing itself in newer learning experiences, achieved through struggle and cultural work.

The experience of the Left theatre and cultural movement in India can be discussed in three phases. The first of these phases begins in the final decade before independence. The second phase covers a period of about 15 years after the declaration of political emergency in 1976. The third and final phase is from the initiation of the economic liberalisation programme under the Narasimha Rao government in the early 1990s up to the present day. Although the primary concern of this book is India after independence, the story of the Left theatre and cultural movement begins in the early 1940s. With the growing tide of anti-Fascism in Europe in the 1930s, the Progressive Writers Association (PWA) was established in 1936, with the aim of forming a 'wide unity' against Fascist aggression. The PWA set up various programmes such as a Peasant Poets' Conference in April 1938 and the Anti-Fascist Writers' and Artists' Association in Bengal in 1938 that included performers working in the jute mills and in the tramways (Pradhan, 1985, 131). On the other hand, the Youth Cultural Institute, established in Calcutta in 1940, consisted mostly of middle-class students and sought to attract the intelligentsia of Calcutta towards the Communists. These efforts culminated in the formation of the IPTA in Bombay in May 1943.

From the very beginning the IPTA formulated its motto as 'people's theatre stars the people', reflecting a desire to work with traditional artists among the peasant and tribal populations, seen to have been neglected by nationalist politicians and the colonial elite. The IPTA's professed aim was to use folk forms and the idioms of the poor to communicate the ideas of Communism and the programmes of the CPI. The IPTA evolved an umbrella all-India structure, with teams in various parts of the country as well as Central Squads that toured extensively. In Andhra Pradesh, the IPTA functioned as the Praja Natya Mandali or PNM (Telugu for 'IPTA') where teams of artists toured the province with songs, dances, plays and bardic recitations. The CPI's large peasant support base in Andhra Pradesh motivated the PNM to use various folk forms like ballad recitations of *burrakatha*, *harikatha* and *pichiguntala* and collective song and dance forms such as *bhajan*, *kolata* and open-air performance *veedhinatakam* (Pradhan, 1985, 306–307). The Bombay IPTA used the performance form *tamasha* even though it was looked down upon as a vulgar form. In fact, the IPTA's use of the *tamasha* became a reason for its respectability. A textile worker, Anna Bhau Sathe, popularised the singing of *powadas* to promote the Communists. In Kerala, artists used temple dance forms like *Ottam Thullal* and militant dance forms like *Poorakali*. Peasant boys and girls danced to the slogans of 'Communist Party Zindabad!' ('Long live the Communist Party!') and '*Kisan Sangham Zindabad*!' ('Long live the Peasants' Association!').

Nabanna, the most well-known production of the pre-independence IPTA, was co-directed by Bijon Bhattacharya and Shombhu Mitra. The play was created out of a need felt by the artists of the Bengal IPTA to create a play to respond to the unprecedented situation in Calcutta where thousands of peasants streamed into the city streets seeking to escape famine-stricken villages and in search for food. However, Calcutta under the colonial administration was not adequately prepared to handle this unprecedented influx of destitute people. Hundreds of people lay dead or disease-ridden in the streets and other public spaces in the city. A section of the Calcutta middle class went about its business without seeking to respond to the scenes of destitution. But another section felt the need to assist the victims and respond to their condition. It was from this need that the IPTA looked to stage a production that explored the politics at the root of the human-made catastrophe – to explain the nature of the colonial state and the character of the Bengali middle class. *Nabanna* presents the story of a group of peasants who are forced to flee to the city in the face of death. But in the city they are confronted by an indifferent section of the middle class who indulge in their wasteful feasts assisted by the ineptitude of the government in curbing the operations of the black market. The production was very well received by Calcutta audiences and was successful in countering the apathy towards the victims of the famine as more volunteers joined the ranks of those who operated the relief camp.

However, the significance of *Nabanna* extended beyond the immediate objectives of famine relief and consolidating the position of the Left. *Nabanna* was created at a time when the Bengali stage was dominated by commercial theatres that survived on religious and mythological plays and around a highly individualised system of star actors. Tickets were usually beyond the reach of ordinary people. The production of *Nabanna* involved actors who were mostly novices or existed outside the circles of the commercial theatres. Moreover, instead of religious and mythological subjects, *Nabanna* presented peasants as the main protagonists. The realistic portrayal of the peasantry meant that the play approximated the everyday language of the characters – a mix of the languages spoken in the Medinipore and Hoogly districts of Bengal – a language that was strange to existing stage practice. Instead of using detailed stage design, the production used jute cloth to mark the set. Locations for specific scenes were indicated by the use of symbols. The use of light and sound also marked a difference from the existing conventions of the commercial stage. Light was used innovatively to project various times of the day and extreme weather conditions on to the stage. We must remember that the IPTA was working with meagre resources, hence the freshness in technical design was the result of ingenuity rather than the employment of the latest technology. Despite adverse criticism from the stalwarts of the Bengali stage, *Nabanna* was very well received by audiences. So much so that it was claimed that, perturbed by the success of *Nabanna*, the owners of the commercial theatres refused to rent out their auditoria to the IPTA for further performances (Sen, 2018, 164). Thus, *Nabanna* marked a break from dominant traditions of the Bengali stage through the choice of subject matter, the realistic depiction onstage, the employment of scenic elements and the abandoning of the star system of the commercial stage. It was the aesthetic freshness brought in by the IPTA and commitment to a politics that sought to respond to many of the problems facing ordinary people and the poor that attracted many young artists towards it. Following the principle of creating a 'wide unity' of artists and intellectuals, the IPTA embraced a wide range of artists, activists and enthusiasts into its fold. While many activists received aesthetic training through their involvement in the IPTA, many artists developed a political stance that was sympathetic to the Communists. Yet there were artists who abjured the commercial stage and preferred working with the IPTA due to the greater artistic freedom the organisation offered.

However, by the late 1940s, the IPTA, as well as the CPI, were embroiled in an ideological confusion that eventually saw the disintegration of the IPTA. The attainment of political independence in 1947 threw the Communists into ideological confusion. The second Congress of the CPI held in Calcutta in

February–March 1948 declared '*Yeh Azadi Jhuta Hai*' ('This independence is a sham' [Roy, 2014, 94]). Under the leadership of B.T. Ranadive, a more stringent line was adopted, calling for an insurrection against the Indian state. We must remember that these developments were occurring against the backdrop of the Chinese Revolution where the Communist Party of China was on the verge of taking power. In India, the peasant armed rebellions of Telengana and the Tebhaga movement were seen by many within the fold of the CPI as signs of the revolution being around the corner. This gave a fillip to left-wing adventurism. In his address at the fourth Conference of the All-India Progressive Writers' Association, Chinmohan Sehanabis 'stressed that all the writers should go to the "front", even at the cost of their writing'. *Marxbadi*, the theoretical journal of the Bengal CPI, repeatedly criticised 'bourgeois' artists who, even as they adopted progressive themes in their work, continued to claim independence for their art (Roy, 2014, 97–98).

Some writers did work within the creative directives of the CPI and shared its distrust of the newly instituted Indian state. In April 1948, Baba Nagarjun wrote an angry untitled poem in Hindi with the first line, '*kagaz ki azadi milti le lo do do aane mein, laal bhavani pargat hui hai suna ki Telengana mein*' ('You can have the paper freedom for two cents, but we have heard the red whirlwind is afoot in Telengana') (Rai, 1984, 33). In the atmosphere of armed confrontation, theatre groups were unable to stage large productions like *Nabanna*, and took to performing guerilla street theatre instead. Such performances would often require the performers to walk from village to village across miles of cultivated land. Performers also had to face police persecution. Yet there were other writers, sincere towards the progressive agenda, who had their commitment questioned by the leadership of the cultural organisations and the CPI. This atmosphere caused a reversal of the 'wide unity' line of the mid-1940s and alienated many writers and artists who had once been attracted to organisations like the IPTA and the PWA.

The CPI's expressed distrust of the Indian government and call for armed rebellion resulted in it being banned. Faced with all-round attack, the CPI corrected its course and adopted a milder stance. It participated in the first national elections held in 1951–1952 and became the largest opposition party. Although the ban on the CPI was lifted and a political line of 'national unity' was adopted, the conditions of distrust within and outside the party did not dissipate. This confusion in assessing the character of the Indian state eventually led to splits in the CPI. The ideological confusion was accentuated by policies adopted by the Indian government under Prime Minister Jawaharlal Nehru. In 1955, at the Avadh session of the Indian National Congress, Nehru outlined his vision of pursuing a path towards a 'socialistic pattern of society' – what was to be known as 'Nehruvian socialism' (Datta, 2008, 22). A section of the CPI called for an agenda of 'National Democracy' and sought to ally with the Nehruvian project in its goal towards socialism. Those who differed formed the Communist Party of India (Marxist) or CPI(M) in 1964. However, in subsequent years, the CPI(M) was to split further to form the Communist Party of India (Maoist-Leninist) and other groups that advocated armed struggle to take on the 'bourgeois-landlord' state. The CPI(M) went on to become the largest among all the Left parties in India, both in terms of strength in the legislatures and among left-wing organisations.

Independence now made possible a state patronage for the arts. In order to determine its policies in the award of grants and encouraging a national agenda for culture, in 1952–1954 the government instituted organisations like the Sangeet Natak Akademi (SNA) for the performing arts, the Lalit Kala Akademi for the fine arts, and the Sahitya Akademi for literature. This now meant that artists no longer had to depend on commercial avenues to pursue and sustain their practice and could look towards the state for support. While state support would open the possibility of greater sustainability of art, it could also hold them to the agenda of the state. The National School of Drama (NSD) was established in 1959. Until then, in the absence of institutional support for theatre training, it was organisations like the IPTA that formed the nursery for emerging actors. Now they could turn to the NSD. Due to the threefold change in scenario in the immediate post-independence period – ideological disarray, intra-organisational sectarianism and the promises held forth by the independent state – the IPTA saw a rapid dissipation of the wide appeal it held among artists and intellectuals. The last all-India conference of the IPTA was held in 1958. Thereafter, the organisation did continue to exist in some states, variously affiliated to the CPI and the CPI(M), but it never regained its all-India character. In fact, no cultural organisation belonging to the Left and matching the spread of the IPTA currently exists in India.

I have argued elsewhere that the going away of the artists – many of whom were to become stalwarts of Indian theatre, cinema, music and other arts for decades to come – severely dented the capacity of the Left to intervene in shaping a progressive and revolutionary culture (Ghosh, 2011). But the impression of the IPTA on the art and entertainment of independent India has far outlived its existence. First, there was the Drama Seminar organised by the SNA in 1956, where leading theatre practitioners from across the country participated in an effort to identify key areas in theatre practice where the Akademi should provide support. One such area was the encouragement of the adaptation of folk performative forms within modern theatrical practice. Termed 'theatre of the roots' by Suresh Awasthi – who later served as the general secretary of the Sangeet Natak Akademi – the scheme sought to address the perceived alienation of urban playwrights from traditional cultural forms. Rustom Bharucha identifies that the term 'folk' 'became popular during the IPTA movement when urban artists were compelled to discover their "roots" in rural cultures' (Bharucha, 2015, 1909). We have already seen how, in their search for an idiom to communicate with the poor and the peasantry, the artists of the IPTA sought to work with traditional cultural forms as well as bringing peasant and working-class artists into their fold. However, it may be noted that the directive of the Drama Seminar was not too far removed from the practice of theatre on the ground where leading Indian playwrights and theatre directors like Habib Tanvir, Utpal Dutt, Vijay Tendulkar and Girish Karnad worked with traditional forms and subjects while infusing them with a contemporary vision. Second, the numerous artists who left the IPTA to work as professionals in theatre, film and other arts continued to infuse a progressive and secular agenda into their art. On the Bengali stage, figures like Shombhu Mitra, even after moving away from the IPTA, laid the foundations of the Naba Natya or Group Theatre movement. What is to be noted is that, since *Nabanna* challenged the dominance of the commercial theatre, the Bengali stage and indeed most theatre in India has remained firmly within the fold of the non-commercial; it remains so even today. Theatre artists, even though they approach their work with full dedication and professionalism, do not earn a living from performing on stage. And this separation of the theatre from the vagaries of the market has allowed it to retain a degree of independence in presenting a critical stance.

The effect of this independence is better understood when seen in contrast to the trajectories of Indian cinema. Many of the erstwhile IPTA writers, singers, musicians and actors went on to pursue careers in the Bombay film industry. Among many popular tropes in popular Hindi films, audiences found a significant presence of progressive themes that drew attention to existing inequalities in society and remained suggestive of a secular polity. The prevalence of progressive themes was most prominent in the 'alternative cinema' or 'parallel cinema' that was supported by grants from the government. The S.K. Patel Film Enquiry Committee, set up by the government for inputs on its intervention into the domain of cinema, submitted its report in 1951. This report and the working of the Film Finance Corporation and later the Films Division sought to secure state investment in creating a branch of the cinema that could work outside the star system that dominated commercial cinema. With a desire to project a progressive and modern face to the world, the government encouraged avant-garde film makers like Mani Kaul, Kumar Shahni, Mrinal Sen and Basu Chatterjee to make films that were critical of different dimensions of Indian society (Datta, 2008, 20–28). This group of filmmakers included people like Ritwik Ghatak, who had emerged from the IPTA movement, Satyajit Ray and Shayam Benegal, who could be said to have worked within the broad contours of a progressive agenda. However, with the liberalisation of the Indian economy in the 1980s and 1990s, state funding for 'parallel cinema' dried up, further constricting these critical voices (Datta, 2008, 15).

It was through the commitment of various artists towards a progressive politics that the Left was able to wield an influence in the field of culture, an influence that was disproportionate to its strength. While many progressive artists operated independently, some of them worked in close coordination with the organisational Left. Habib Tanvir (1923–2009) began his association with theatre with the Bombay IPTA in the 1940s where he participated in 'agit-prop plays done on an improvised stage in open-air [*sic*] for thousands of workers' (Katyal, 2012, 18–19). Tanvir's experience with the IPTA and the PWA heightened his sensitivity towards the language used by the common man. It was this experience that drew him to his association with Chattisgarhi *nacha* actors and Chattisgarhi traditional forms and techniques. The Naya Theatre he founded was a symbiotic experience where Tanvir learnt from the Chattisgarhi actors and guided them to evoke contemporary subjects in plays. Much of his work – notably, *Charandas Chor* (*Charandas the Thief*, 1975), *Ponga Pandit* (*The Fraudulent Priest*, 1976),

86 *Arjun Ghosh*

Moteram ka Satyagrah (*Moteram's Fast Unto Death*, 1988), *Sadak* (*Road*, 1994) and *Zahareeli Hawa* (*Bhopal*, 2002) – presents sharp critiques of bigotry, religious fundamentalism and crony capitalism (Deshpande, 2004).[3]

Utpal Dutt's association with the IPTA was much shorter than that of Tanvir. When the CPI was banned, Dutt's group, the Little Theatre Group (LTG), included a short piece in its programme protesting the action. At that time the LTG produced English plays, primarily Shakespeare, for an upper-middle-class Calcutta audience. Gradually, Dutt and his colleagues understood the disjuncture between their radical stance and their engagement with English plays. Dutt joined the IPTA in 1950. There he worked on street-corner agit-prop productions like *Chargesheet* (1950) to mobilise public opinion against the imprisonment of Communist leaders. But these were also times of internal strife within the CPI. Dutt's outspokenness and non-acceptance of dogmatic Marxism were looked upon as dissidence. He was 'eased out of the organisation' (Dutt, 1982, 36; Bharucha, 1983, 56–61). But his association with the Communists continued. In 1962 the LTG produced *The Special Train*, an agit-prop play that sought to expose a nexus between industrialists and the ruling party against striking workers. The play is said to have worked in favour of the Communists in the 1962 elections and was attacked by strongmen of the ruling party (Bharucha, 1983, 69–70). The LTG now gave way to the People's Little Theatre in 1969. Dutt turned his attention to the *jatra* form and used it to further political themes. This move was not without controversies as the mainstream Bengali theatre considered *jatra* to be an inferior form. With his characteristic sharpness, Dutt replied to his critics: 'this goes on everywhere; they write, they speak against *jatra*. Why? Because the *jatra* has huge audiences, they have none' (Dutt, 1984, 34). In 1975 Dutt produced *Barricade* which presented an allegorical story of the Nazis rigging the 1933 German elections and framing the Communists in false cases to seize power. The action clearly pointed the finger at the Congress party which was accused of rigging the 1972 elections to the West Bengal state assembly (Bharucha, 1983, 102–103). Dutt's next play *Dushopner Nagari* (*City of Nightmares*, 1974) abandoned the allegorical framework and directly accused the ruling party of murdering Communists. The performances were attacked by 'Congress gangsters', the crew was assaulted and the set was smashed. On one particular occasion, a performance of *Dushopner Nagari* was defended by members of CPI(M) by barricading the routes leading to the theatre (Dutt, 1982, 33–34). Although Dutt was a partisan, he did not abandon his artistic and intellectual freedom to critique.

The attacks on *Dushopner Nagari* were symptomatic of the growing authoritarianism of the Indian state. The promise of a progressive and egalitarian state that was held out in the phase of 'Nehruvian Socialism' wore out and gave way to increasing discontent and opposition that threatened the uninterrupted rule of the Congress party. Along with various mass organisations that sprouted in the early 1970s were theatre groups that sought to revive the legacy of the IPTA. The most significant among them was the Jana Natya Manch (Janam) which was put together by a group of student activists in Delhi in 1973. Until the proclamation of internal emergency in 1976, the actors of Janam would perform progressive proscenium plays on makeshift stages in working-class areas in and around

Delhi. Their shows were hosted by various working-class organisations allied to the CPI(M). The proclamation of emergency was used by the government to suppress dissent, imprison leaders of the opposition and smash the fighting capacities of mass organisations. Thus, after the emergency was lifted, Janam found that, although the trade unions and other fighting organisations needed Janam's plays to regroup, they could no longer generate enough resources to hire the stage, lights and sound required for the performances. It was at that point in 1978, during brainstorming by the Janam members, that Safdar Hashmi – one of the founding members of the group – suggested 'if we can't take big plays to the people then we will take short ones' (Hashmi, 1997, 58–59). With the performance of *Machine* (1978), Janam undertook an exhilarating journey that saw street theatre become the most prevalent form of communication for various grassroots organisations.

The struggle against the excesses of the emergency brought about a significant transformation of the Indian polity. For the first time a non-Congress coalition assumed power in New Delhi. In West Bengal the Left Front, led by the CPI(M), came to power in what was to be an uninterrupted stint continuing for 33 years. Outside electoral politics, the upsurge against the emergency saw an outburst of popular rebellion giving birth to numerous mass organisations, notably among women and the oppressed castes. In the 10 years between 1978 and 1988, Janam performed 4,300 times, presenting 22 different plays in 90 cities and seen by over 2.5 million people (Hashmi, 1989, 13). In Karnataka the cultural organisation Samudaya performed its first street play – Krishnaswamy's *Belchi* (1978) – a work based on the killings of Dalit agricultural labourers in Belchi, Bihar. *Belchi* was not only performed across Karnataka. It has also been translated and performed in several Indian languages (Deshpande, 1997, 13). Similar groups also shaped up in various states across the country wherever Left organisations were involved in mobilising people against exploitation and religious extremism. In Punjab, Gursharan Singh and his fellow artists performed *Takht Lahore* (*The Throne of Lahore*, 1975) and *Bund Kamre* (*Closed Doors*, 1976), efforts that landed him in jail. Allied to the CPI(M), Singh took to theatre against terrorist threats at the height of separatism in Punjab with *Sadharan Log* (*Common People*, 1981), *Dharam Mamla Nij Da* (*Religion Is a Private Matter*, 1982) and *Baba Bolda Hai* (*The Old Man Speaks*, 1985). In Delhi, women's groups like Theatre Union took to street plays like *Om Swaha* (*Unholy Offerings*, 1979) to mobilise public opinion against dowry deaths and other atrocities concerning women (Mangai, 2015, 42). There were many women's groups performing street theatre in various parts of the country. Although most of these groups were not organisationally aligned to any political party, the progressive agenda of their plays and their choice of the street theatre form worked towards a transformation of values that would benefit the Left movement.

Most of the street theatre groups mentioned up to now worked from urban spaces with their actors emerging from the urban middle classes who underwent ideological training through their activism and theatre work. In Andhra Pradesh we find examples of two groups whose work predominantly existed in rural and tribal spaces. The Praja Natya Mandali (PNM) – aligned to the CPI(M) – works among agricultural workers and Dalits. By the year 2000 it had developed an immense network of over 1100 branches with over 22,000 members. Devi, one of the stalwarts of the PNM, calls our attention to the involvement of theatre activists in taking on discriminatory caste practices in rural Andhra Pradesh (Devi, 2008). Functioning within the territory of Andhra Pradesh is the Jana Natya Mandali. Founded in 1972, it is a cultural group aligned to the CPI (Maoist) (Gadar, 2002, 9).[4] The CPI (Maoist) being a banned organisation, the Jana Natya Mandali has to function undercover. At various times in its history, the Mandali created armed troupes of artists to move through forests to perform among predominantly tribal audiences. As loud singing and dancing could potentially attract the attention of the police, the Mandali relied mostly on poetry and stories. One of the most popular figures emerging from the Mandali is Gadar, a popular poet and balladeer who has used *burrakatha* and various folk forms to articulate the ideology of People's War. The Jana Natya Mandali has been particularly successful in appropriating folk form and tunes to the revolutionary cause. This has been proven in times when the ban was lifted on Maoist organisations and they organised open rallies which saw enormous congregations of people, particularly for the cultural performances.

The period of the second upsurge of people's theatre and cultural movements, which began during the mass revolt against the internal emergency, slowly ebbed away from the early 1990s when the Indian government chose the path of neoliberal economic reform. But before that, January 1989 saw the murder of Safdar Hashmi, the convenor of the Jana Natya Manch, while Janam was performing the street play *Halla Bol (Attack)* at Sahibabad near Delhi. Hashmi was killed by gangsters close to the ruling Congress party. His death and funeral saw an unprecedented coming-together of artists and workers who mourned the demise of an artist who had dedicated his life to the cause of a progressive Communist politics. Hashmi's murder saw a surge in the number of groups across the country that started performing street theatre. The formation of the Safdar Hashmi Memorial Trust (SAHMAT) saw the formation of a cross-section of artists and cultural workers, perhaps the largest such platform since the disintegration of the IPTA. However, the impact of the activities of SAHMAT has been no match to that of the IPTA. The fate of street theatre and the cultural organisations of the Left was tied to the trajectory of the Left movement in India. The policies of liberalisation, privatisation and globalisation (LPG), unleashed from 1991, have resulted in the reassertion of capitalist hegemony over the working class: greater casualisation of labour has taken away the capacities of collective bargaining (Prashad, 2015). At the same time, the demolition of the Babri Mosque at Ayodhya in 1992 marked the historic rise of the Hindu Right and an ascendancy of identitarian politics.

While these developments have made the task of organising labour more difficult for the Communists, they have made the task of cultural organisations difficult as well. For instance, the demand to create a separate state of Telengana – to be carved out of Andhra Pradesh – made the work of the Praja Natya Mandali difficult as the CPI(M) opposed the bifurcation of the state. In Delhi, the dwindling strength of the Left meant that the Jana Natya Manch found that the logistical support it could derive from the CPI(M) and its allied organisations became hard to come by. The period since the 1990s also saw the increased intervention of non-governmental organisations (NGOs) in addressing issues arising out of the social sector. NGOs, as well as various government agencies, adopted street theatre as a medium to reach out to their target audiences. This gave rise to a structure where street theatre artists would contract out their labour in the service of specific campaign messages. This structure created an iteration of street theatre that was stripped of the politics of critiquing exploitative and unjust structures. It no longer sought to empower people in their struggle against oppression. Rather, it identified the fault with the people themselves and sought to reform them (Ghosh, 2005). The LPG policies have also resulted in a gradual withdrawal of the state from various social sectors as well as from support for arts and culture. This has impeded the independent functioning of artists. We have also seen how the reduction in support for independent filmmakers stifled 'parallel cinema'. The accompanying emphasis upon commercialising entertainment has largely relied on jingoistic and conservative themes and abjured critical stances.

In this period the Left found itself embroiled in internal debates regarding its approach towards neo-liberal policies. While the CPI(M) gave up a 'historic' opportunity to lead a coalition government in 1996, it led the government in the state of West Bengal and aggressively pursued pro-market policies in the 2000s. As in 1942, the Left now finds itself in a quandary. The instances of exploitation in India have only grown stronger in the post-LPG phase; income disparities have increased with conditions pointing towards the relevance of a Left politics in India today. However, the Indian Communist parties have not been able to come up with any fresh ideas that could tap into the discontent and energies of the people. In the first phase of the Left cultural movement, the innovations of the IPTA helped it gain acceptability and counter political isolation. The energies of that phase remained effective for about three decades. The second phase was the period of ferment in which grassroots activists took their politics to wider audiences through a street theatre revolution. In each of these phases, the innovations were not arrived at through interventions made by the Communist leadership, but through innovations undertaken by ideologically committed artists. But the popular support and outreach brought about by these innovations benefited the Left movement. Even in a period of crisis today, very committed groups of artists and activists continue to function within the fold of the Left. Outside of cultural groups, the Left organisations continue to lead some important movements that have seen mass participation in the recent past. Whether any of these efforts will lead to a revival of the Left in India will be answered by history. The Left in India awaits an IPTA-like movement that can consolidate the people's discontent.

Notes

1 I refer to the Communist Party of India (Marxist) or CPI(M), the Communist Party of India (CPI), the Forward Bloc, and the Revolutionary Socialist Party (RSP) amongst a few other parties.
2 The Left parties, led by the CPI(M), have held the government in West Bengal uninterrupted from 1977. The Left has also ruled Tripura since 1977, except between 1988

and 1993. While the Left did win back the Kerala state government in 2016, it lost in Tripura in 2018.
3 Much of Tanvir's work should be seen as collaboration with his actors – be it with the Nacha actors of the Naya Theatre or other groups. *Moteram ka Satyagrah* was adapted by Safdar Hashmi from a short story by Munshi Premchand and was performed under Tanvir's direction by the actors of the Jana Natya Manch. *Ponga Pandit* has been performed by various groups since the 1930s. *Zahreeli Hawa* was written by Rahul Verma.
4 The CPI (Maoist) was formed in 2004 by the merger of the CPI (Marxist-Leninist) People's War Group, the CPI (Marxist-Leninist) Party Unity, and the Maoist Communist Centre.

Works cited

Bharucha, Rustom (1983). *Rehearsals of Revolution: The Political Theater of Bengal*. Honolulu, HI: University of Hawaii Press.
Bharucha, Rustom (2015). 'Notes on the Invention of Tradition'. *Economic and Political Weekly*, 24(33), 7–8.
Bhattacharya, Bijon (2018). *Nabanna: Of Famine and Resilience: A Play* (orig. publ. 1944), trans. Arjun Ghosh. New Delhi: Rupa.
Damodaran, Sumangala (2017). *The Radical Impulse: Music in the Tradition of the Indian People's Theatre Association*. New Delhi: Tulika Books.
Datta, Sangeeta (2008). *Shayam Benegal*. New Delhi: Roli Books.
Deshpande, Sudhanva (1997). '"The Inexhaustible Work of Criticism in Action": Street Theatre of the Left'. *Seagull Theatre Quarterly*, 16, 3–22.
Deshpande, Sudhanva (2004). 'Upside-Down Midas: Habib Tanvir at 80'. *The Drama Review*, 48(4), 71–80.
DEVI (2008.) 'Response'. Not the Drama Seminar, Ninasam, Heggoddu, Karnataka organised by the India Theatre Forum, 22–26 March 2008 (online). Available from: http://test.theatreforum.in/static/upload/docs/DEVI.pdf (accessed 18 Oct 2018).
Dutt, Utpal (1982). *Towards a Revolutionary Theatre*. Calcutta: M.C. Sarkar.
Dutt, Utpal (1984). 'An Armoured Car on the Road to Proletarian Revolution'. Interview with Malini Bhattacharya and Mihir Bhattacharya. *Journal of Arts and Ideas*, 8, 25–42.
Gadar (2002). *The Voice of Liberation*. Secunderabad: Janam Pata.
Ghosh, Arjun (2005). 'Theatre for the Ballot: Campaigning with Street Theatre in India'. *The Drama Review*, 49(4), 171–182.
Ghosh, Arjun (2011). 'Challenges, Innovations and Commitment: Cultural Intervention and Cultural Resistance'. *Economic and Political Weekly*, 46(24), 69–75.
Ghosh, Arjun (2018). 'Introduction'. In: Bijon Bhattacharya (ed.), *Nabanna: Of Famine and Resilience: A Play*, trans. Arjun Ghosh. New Delhi: Rupa, pp. 1–27.
Hashmi, Moloyashree (1997). 'Drama Has to Be Created and Crafted, Even on the Streets'. Interview with Anjum Katyal. *Seagull Theatre Quarterly*, 16, 57–71.
Hashmi, Safdar (1989). *Right to Perform: Selected Writings of Safdar Hashmi*. New Delhi: SAHMAT.
Katyal, Anjum (2012). *Habib Tanvir: Towards an Inclusive Theatre*. New Delhi: Sage.
Mangai, A. (2015). *Acting Up: Gender and Theatre in India, 1979 Onwards*. New Delhi: LeftWord.
Pradhan, Sudhi (1985). *Marxist Cultural Movement in India: Chronicles and Documents*. Calcutta: Santi Pradhan.

Prashad, Vijay (2015). *No Free Left: The Futures of Indian Communism*. New Delhi: LeftWord.
Rahim, N.K. (1969). 'Dharti ke Lal'. *Bohurupee: Nabanna Special Issue*, 33, 125.
Rai, Alok (1984). 'The Trauma of Independence: Some Aspects of Progressive Hindi Literature 1945–47'. *Journal of Arts and Ideas*, 6, 19–34.
Roy, Anuradha (2014). *Cultural Communism in Bengal: 1936–1952*. Delhi: Primus.
Sarkar, Sumit (1983). *Modern India, 1885–1947*. New Delhi: Macmillan.
Sen, Sova (2018). 'Nabanna and Me'. In: Bijon Bhattacharya, *Nabanna: Of Famine and Resilience: A Play*, trans. Arjun Ghosh. New Delhi: Rupa, pp. 163–169.

6 Contested natures and tribal identities
Regional nationalism as ethnography – rereading Rajam Krishnan's *When the Kurinji Blooms*

Anita Balakrishnan

Noted Tamil writer Rajam Krishnan (1925–2014) was known for her exhaustively researched social novels that depicted characters that were rarely seen in the Tamil fiction of the time. Her prolific literary output included 40 novels, two biographies, 20 plays and several short stories that focused on the socially marginalised: impoverished farmers, tribal people, fisherfolk, jungle dacoits and female labourers. She is considered to be a pathbreaker in Tamil writing for the anthropological and ethnographic research that she undertook before she wrote about a region and its inhabitants.

Krishnan's fiction is unabashedly didactic, with her characters often voicing the author's own views on social reform and serving to emphasise her penchant for reshaping society. She became interested in the tribespeople of the Nilgiris region in south-western Tamil Nadu when she lived there for a few years with her engineer husband. She spoke of the difficulty of depicting the changes in the lives of the tribals and their resistance to sharing intimate details of their lives with strangers. Another well-known Tamil writer, Ambai, has recorded the meticulousness of Krishnan's research that would equal any trained ethnographer's methods.

An ethnographer typically goes out into the field and lives closely with the people for an extended period of time, observing social interactions, customs and rituals. Ethnographers were traditionally considered to be able to convey an objective, unmediated reality. However, James Clifford (1986) radically altered the understanding and practice of ethnography, arguing that ethnographies were 'inventions' of culture 'made or fashioned' (6). The ethnographer is no longer a neutral, unprejudiced observer: he or she makes decisions on which people to observe, how actions are to be interpreted, what is seen as significant, as well as ways in which the ethnographer's presence impacts on the actions of the observed. Ethnographers also structure the ways in which they communicate their findings. Recent postcolonial critiques have engaged with issues of power relations within research, challenging the ways in which ethnography and anthropology have been enmeshed within the exploitative relations of colonial enterprise. Colonial anthropologists' depictions of the tribespeople of the Nilgiris region show significant differences. While an early observer notes their frank deportment, their well-proportioned and muscular appearance, and their freedom from servility, a later account records the absence of any shame or religious belief and their inability to control their passions. As Gunnel Cederlöf and K. Sivaramakrishnan (2006) note, 'the two decades that span these two accounts saw a dramatic change in polity, man–land relationships and systems of authority and rule' (66). These were also the years that saw the changeover from the East India Company as an enterprise of traders and administrators to administrators and rulers of conquered territory.

Krishnan in her detailed narrative presents the Badagas as a people who treasure their traditions, culture and land. The Badaga tribe was an agrarian community who lived in the Nilgiris and practised dairy farming besides raising food crops. They migrated to the Nilgiris about two centuries ago due to famine, political turmoil and oppression in the Mysore region. Although they had earlier practised subsistence farming, the Badagas gradually switched over to cash crops such as tea and coffee under colonial rule. This led to a transformation in their lifestyles, habits, customs and even their nutritional patterns. The radical shift in consumption and production patterns fostered destabilising social forces that ultimately served to completely obliterate the tribe's distinctive culture that was based on living harmoniously within their ecosystem.

The British strategy for the development of India was based on the adoption of policies that would provide law and order, the development of foreign trade based on the free trade principle and the investment of capital. A small number of Indians were selectively educated to assist in these functions, but the vast majority of Indians were denied access to modern technology. The British believed that the logic of private gain, individual enterprise and market forces would take care of development and economic growth. By the late 18th and early 19th century, the British had remodelled Indian agrarian relations on the theory that private property in the hands of the landowners or farmers would lead to agricultural development. But in practice this led to the landlords renting their lands at exorbitant rates to peasants, leaving them to the mercy of moneylenders which led to widespread famines. The powerful colonial state apparatus exerted great pressure on poor peasants, undermining the well-organised village-level systems of management and self-governance. Furthermore, the British were focused on exploiting the forest resources and agricultural surplus to be exported to Britain to fuel that nation's rapidly developing economy.

British officials saw the promotion of foreign trade as another major instrument for India's development. They encouraged farmers to raise cash crops such as indigo, jute, cotton and tea that would find ready markets in England and Europe. This had the unexpected consequence of altering time-honoured agricultural traditions and practices leading to the loss of unique folkways and rituals, thereby undermining the farmers' close connection to the land. Frantz Fanon writes on the psychology of colonised peoples in his seminal work *The Wretched of the Earth* (1961). He asserts that for colonised people, the most essential and concrete value is the land which will bring them bread and above all dignity. Land as a fundamental entity that shapes life is a perspective that is common to both the coloniser and the colonised. But because the colonisers placed their homeland above all else, the rest of the world's environment had to be conquered and controlled according to the conscience of the colonisers. As Richard Grove (1995) notes,

> the kind of homogenising capital-intensive transformation of people, trade, economy and environment with which we are familiar today can be traced back at least as far as the beginnings of European colonial expansion, as the agents of new European capital and urban markets sought to extend their areas of operation and sources of raw materials.
>
> (2)

This ecological imperialism is what Alfred Crosby (2015) understands to be the reason behind many environmental changes.

The transformation of colonised lands into an imitation of the imperialists' homelands was part of the superego of the colonisers. They imbued the material features of their mother country with quasi-ethical qualities. This led to the colonisers' overruling of regionalised conservation techniques and their contempt for the intimate knowledge of a region that tribal people possessed. This led to the unceasing transformation of the natural world into the world of artificial fabrications such as roads, buildings and plantations and this had the most serious implications for large sections of Indian society. Most of the poor who scratch the earth and pray for rains to grow enough food to fill their bellies and build their own huts with bamboo daubed with mud were adversely affected by the changes wrought by colonialism and its aftermath. Such people depend on their immediate environment to meet their everyday needs; environmentalists Madhav Gadgil and Ramachandra Guha (1995) call them 'ecosystem people' (4). Under pressure from such capitalist-driven forces, the natural world continued to recede, reducing its capacity to support these people. Dams, mines and industries have physically displaced large numbers of ecosystem people, reducing them to ecological refugees, people living on the margins of islands of urban prosperity who can no longer depend on the land and forest resources to support them and who lack the purchasing power to obtain the commodities available in the shops. The capitalist economy introduced by the British led to the ecosystem people and ecological refugees being exposed to resource omnivores, as Gadgil and Guha (1995) term them (4), urban elites who commanded the economic, social and political power to demand more than their fair share of natural resources. Both during the colonial era and after independence, these urban professionals – doctors, lawyers, bankers, employees in government and government-aided organisations, and wealthy farmers – had the purchasing power to buy cars, wear fashionable clothes, and consume foods from all corners of the land. They became the chief beneficiaries of state development policies and they continue to pay subsidised rates for the electricity and water they consume that is brought to them from many kilometres away. This threefold classification of ecosystem people, ecological refugees and omnivores, as Gadgil and Guha (1995) admit, does have boundary problems, but it enables a convincing interpretation of economic and environmental change in India.

Despite its global relevance and prominence in public discourse, environmentalism has not been able to significantly impact development policy in India. Although a prudent, sustainable use of India's environmental resources is in the interest of the majority of India's population, the history of Western colonialism and industrial development has benefited only a tiny elite while inflicting tremendous environmental violence. The battles being fought over the environment in India today have as their focus the conflict between ecosystem people and the rural sector and the powerful resource omnivores who have access to political circles. For instance, in the 1940s and 1950s, politicians, particularly Jawaharlal Nehru, were drawn to river valley development as a practical manifestation of the contribution modern science could make towards building a 'new India'. The speech Nehru made at the inauguration of the Nangal portion of the Bhakra project has become famous for its description of Indian dams as 'temples of a New Age', as Daniel Klingensmith notes in his study of the Damodar Valley Corporation (2007, 263). Although Nehru unquestionably had an abiding belief in modern technology for its own sake, his commitment to dam projects had a practical dimension as well. Like many of his contemporaries, Nehru believed that India's future stability depended on achieving Western-style material affluence through heavy industrialisation, which in turn would require increased supplies of power and water. Such projects also served to legitimate the state and its claims – but only among the professional, English-educated elite classes. Nehru and other politicians, who were themselves a part of this class and constituency, capitalised on the elite's dominant status in society to legitimate development that served the interests of this class. However, peasant struggles and ecological battles have shown that grassroots movements can be effective in subverting invasive development such as dams, large-scale trawler fishing, and commercial forest operations. As Guha and Joan Martinez Alier (1997) note, Indian environmental movements seek to wrest control of nature from the powerful commercial–industrial sector and place it in the control of rural communities who live within that space but are denied access to it. These communities often subsist on produce from their surrounding areas and their demands on the environment are less damaging. They can also draw on their accumulated cultural traditions and local ecological wisdom to manage the grasslands, forests and rivers on a sustainable basis. As colonial and post-colonial capitalist expansion has caused a dangerous loss of natural resources, any attempt to restore these resources must draw on alternative environmental activism as well.

The contrast between a Western environmentalism with its emphasis on the preservation of pristine wilderness areas to serve as a refuge from the consumerist lifestyle of the cities and the activism of the disempowered rural people seeking the right to live in their ancestral lands, practise their culture and pursue their agricultural methods is striking. Guha and Martinez Alier dramatically term this the opposition between the 'full stomach environmentalism' of the North and the 'empty belly environmentalism' of the South (1997, 12). Rob Nixon (2011) has also termed such insidious appropriation of natural resources by commercial interests as an example of 'slow violence or environmentalism of the poor' (2).

The environmental movement of the poor in India has been the preserve of rural communities – farmers, fisherfolk, pastoralists and shifting cultivators – in response to the takeover by the state or private companies of the common property they depend on for their livelihood. The transformation of India into a wasteland, which began during colonial rule, has been continued by post-independence governments.

As Cederlöf and Sivaramakrishnan (2006) observe, after India gained independence from the British, the ruling elite continued the colonial policy of annexing tribal and community lands, citing the national interest. Celebrations of the nation and assertions of nationhood appropriated nature to manifest the legitimacy of such claims. As has been discussed earlier, metropolitan–secular nationalisms premised on geographical distance and cultural differences, which needed to be traversed and transcended in the formation of the nation-state, had their strongest supporter in Nehru. In the romantic naturalism of the newly independent nation, the figure of the Adivasi or indigenous person of South Asia was contrasted with images of devastated nature to reflect India's state under British rule. Yet during Nehru's tenure as prime minister, natural resources were diverted towards large-scale transformation of the landscape in the name of developing the modern Indian nation. In this, there was remarkable convergence between the colonial and post-colonial states with both depicting a romantic vision of the landscape while transforming it radically. Nehru has been widely criticised by environmental historians for the ecologically disastrous manifestations of his development vision seen in large dams, industrial pollution and nuclear proliferation.

Explaining his use of the phrase 'slow violence', Nixon (2011) contends that violence is generally conceived as an action or event that is immediate in time and spectacular and explosive in space. However, he believes that there is the need to engage with a different kind of violence, one that is neither spectacular nor instantaneous, but incremental and accretive. The repercussions of such violence become apparent either in the short term or appear after a long lapse of time. Nixon calls for the need to engage with a range of representational, narrative and strategic challenges posed by the relative invisibility of slow violence. Climate change, disappearing forests and bodies of water, thawing polar regions, and several other environmental catastrophes offer representational obstacles that hinder our efforts to act decisively. Narratives such as Krishnan's novel *When the Kurinji Blooms* that focus on a past where tribes lived in harmony with nature are an attempt to address such challenges.

The principal casualties of such insidious ecological violence are the poor: those lacking either social or political leverage. These ecosystem people depend so heavily upon the biosphere for fuel, fodder and food that when it is damaged or compromised, they are the most affected for they cannot access any alternative means of procuring their everyday needs. The effects of their unseen poverty are worsened by the invisibility of such ecological damage that seeps into many of their lives. The media bias towards the spectacular and the sensational worsens the vulnerability of ecosystems that are treated as disposable by commercial–industrial interests while simultaneously increasing the susceptibility of the poor who, as Nixon (2011) observes, become 'disposable people' (21).

Contested natures and tribal identities 97

It is against such interlinked ecological and human disposability that a resurgent environmentalism of the poor has emerged, particularly across the global South. At this juncture, it should be noted that the poor are by no means a homogeneous entity: they have almost infinite local variations along vectors of race, ethnicity, class and region. When these heterogeneous communities are subject to the robust, unrelenting pressures of commerce and development, their cohesiveness and resilience are tested. This raises certain questions: how much coercion and bribery can the community withstand? How can a poor tribal community control the mix of subsistence and market strategies it deploys in its attempt to survive? How can that community negotiate its right to follow its own culture when faced with bulldozers and moneymen?

It is well known that, as Nixon (2010) argues, the narrative of 'a modern nation-state is sustained by the production of imagined communities but also by the active production of unimagined communities' (62). The narratives of disempowered communities that disturb the implied trajectory of national ascent are suppressed or silenced by 'energetically inculcated habits of imaginative limit ... the direct violence of physical eviction [of such communities] becomes coupled to an indirect bureaucratic and media violence that creates and sustains the conditions for successfully administered invisibility' (Nixon, 2010, 62). These people who have been rendered invisible may be called 'development refugees' (Thayer Scudder cited in Nixon, 2010, 63). Nixon (2010) observes that when these refugees are severed from ecosystems that have nurtured them from time immemorial, they are 'stranded not just in place but in time as well' (72): that is, from memories of their ancestors. When a dam displaces people from a region which has 'shaped the agricultural ... and nutritional dynamics of a community' (Nixon, 2010, 72–73) – indeed their very culture – it ruptures the cultural ethos of the tribe.

To justify this egregious violence, bureaucrats and commercial interests employ three strategies: direct violence, a rhetorical appeal to selective self-sacrifice (your loss is for the greater good), and a suggestion that the culture of the displaced is inferior. It was perhaps in relation to such attitudes that Krishnan wrote her meticulously researched, lyrical Tamil novel *Kurinjithen* (1962), translated into English in 2002 as *When the Kurinji Blooms*, that celebrates the distinctive culture and historical background of the Badaga tribe. Krishnan's novel is a family saga of three generations of Badagas, ranging from Lingayya, the grandfather, to Jogi, his son, and Nanjan, the grandson. It is set in a typical Badaga *hatti*, or village, at a time when the hillsides in the Nilgiris were covered with *kurinji* flowers every 12 years. In the novel, the Badagas lead a peaceful and contented life following their customary agricultural practices, taking pleasure in tilling the soil, and growing their own food.

The novel opens with Jogi as a nine-year-old boy, who revels in the simple life of the *hatti*. Although some of his playmates attend the local village school, Jogi does not; instead he is content to spend his days tending his father's cattle. As he grows into adulthood, the Badaga's peaceful life, cultivating *ragi, samai* and potatoes for food, is drastically altered. The people who had no taste for money and who were contented with their simple lives begin cultivating tea in imitation of the British planters. Their sole objective in this endeavour is to amass wealth and live in a grand style like the British colonisers. The traditions of the tribe begin to fade and families who were once united grow apart and become adversaries. Jogi's family, who cling to the old ways, become impoverished, while the family of Kariamallar, who start planting tea, prosper. The construction of the Pykara dam on their mountains strikes a death knell for Badaga culture. The Nilgiris occupy the meeting place of the Western and Eastern Ghats. There are more than 400 tribal villages in the Nilgiris with each tribe practising unique customs and traditions. The many dam projects across the rivers in the region have submerged vast areas of forest. The Pykara is one of the biggest streams in the region that eventually flows into the River Cauvery. The Pykara hydroelectric project was one of the first dam projects in Tamil Nadu. The project, which was initiated in 1929, was meant to generate electricity for the industries in the region. Krishnan's evocation of tribal life reveals the devastating impact of this dam project on the lives of the tribespeople in the area. Jogi's family, once proud leaders in the community, displaced from their ancestral village due to the expansion of the local school, are ousted again by the dam construction project and are reduced to the status of 'development refugees'.

Although the narration is omniscient, it is through Jogi's consciousness that the narrative is refracted, revealing his significance in the novel. In the first few chapters, Jogi as a young boy is enthralled by the beauty of his birthplace, Maragathamalai or 'emerald mountain', and hopes to spend all his days raising dairy cows and working on the land. In their preface, Uma Narayanan and Prema Seetharam, the English translators of *When the Kurinji Blooms*, describe the living conditions of the tribe:

> The Badagas live in extensive villages or *hattis* composed of rows of thatched or tiled houses. Each house is partitioned into an outer room (*edumane*) and an inner one (*ogamane*). If the family owns cattle, a portion of the *ogamane* in converted into a milk-house (*hagottu*). The one who milks the cow wears freshly washed (*madi*) clothes. The milk is collected in a long cylindrical vessel made out of bamboo (*honai*).
>
> (ix)

The significance of dairy farming in the culture is seen in the very design of their dwellings. For the Badagas, cattle-rearing and milking are considered to be auspicious activities reflecting the importance accorded to cattle in their culture.

The simple pleasures that provide a sense of contentment in Lingayya's household are missing in his elder brother's family. His elder brother's son Rangan, in contrast to Jogi, is embittered with his lot. He dreams of surreptitiously running away to Othai, the nearest town, to seek his fortune there. When Rangan is selected by Lingayya to tend to the fire in the Hethappa temple, he rebels and escapes to Othai. Jogi is then asked to step in as the caretaker of the temple and he does so happily. For years Jogi performs his tasks in the temple assiduously.

When he emerges from the temple after seven years he finds his world altered radically. Lingayya, a hardworking farmer, had raised food crops like *ragi* and *samai* and shared the surplus with the neighbouring *hattis*. The family had a small patch of land next to their house. When Jogi emerges from the temple, he finds his father is sickly and unable to farm the land. This is a narrative suggesting that the winds of change are gradually encroaching upon the traditional habits and folkways of the Badagas. An elegiac tone pervades the novel indicating the declining fortunes of the tribe, who lose their ancestral land, their distinctive way of life, and their sense of community due to the effects of colonial development.

However, Krishnan does not necessarily espouse a regressive, anti-modern way of life in her celebration of Badaga traditions through her protagonist, Jogi. At times, Jogi is repelled by some of the crude traditions of the tribe. When his father dies, his uncle Madhan invites the Kothar tribe, who play their lively music on their unique musical instruments. Madhan dons colourful silk and satin skirts and begins to dance enthusiastically to the catchy Kothar music with others. Jogi in his grief is unable to bear this gaiety at a funeral ceremony. He is supported in this by the young educated Badaga men, Krishnan and Arjunan. The tribal elders are aghast at this breaking of tradition but Jogi's will prevails. Nevertheless, an elaborate nine-tiered funeral car is prepared for Lingayya as befitting his status as an honoured elder and he is laid to rest.

The title of the novel is significant, for when the *kurinji* blooms, the lives of the tribal people are filled with peace and contentment. The blooming of the *kurinji* flower once every 12 years has great symbolic meaning for the Badagas as traditionally they have measured time in terms of the flowering of the *kurinji* bush. As development projects begin to alter the Nilgiris ecosystem, resulting in a drastic change in the environment, the flowering cycle of the *kurinji* plant is disrupted. This is reflected in the radical changes that occur in Lingayya's household, with the family becoming impoverished over time. Jogi imbibes his father's cultural ethos and develops a deep reverence for the land he owned and for Badaga folkways. Krishnan, the elder son of the landowner Kariamallar, adapts to modern ways, acquiring education and gradually developing his lands into a thriving tea plantation.

Rangan, Jogi's cousin, is an interesting character whose life seems to be placed in counterpoint to those of Krishnan and Jogi. Since early childhood Rangan has been contemptuous of the rustic life of the Badagas, dreaming of a luxurious life in Othai where the British established tea plantations and local government. The product of a broken home, Rangan is always envious of Jogi's happy family home and Krishnan's affluence. Kariamalla, Krishnan's grandfather, is a *maniakkarar* or wealthy farmer. In contrast to the hardworking and caring Lingayya, Madhan, Rangan's father, is a lazy alcoholic who wastes no time or effort on his second wife or children. The disgruntled Rangan runs away to Othai at the first opportunity. Here he tries to translate his childhood dreams into reality. He uses unscrupulous means to earn money and succeeds to an extent, buying some land and growing potatoes. When Rangan hears that Krishnan and Paru are in love, he rushes back to Maragathamalai to assert his claim over Paru as she is his intended wife, according to the customs of the tribe. This creates a feud between the Kariamalla family and Jogi's family. Once Rangan marries Paru, however, he neglects her and the marriage is unhappy. When Rangan is unfaithful to her, Paru leaves him and taking her two daughters with her, she moves back into Jogi's house. Due to the intensity of the feud, Krishnan does not inoculate Paru's daughters and they die in an outbreak of disease. Meanwhile Rangan acquires lands in Othai but lacks the commitment and patience to farm the land properly. He also begins to drink and gamble in the horseraces, losing much of his money in the process. When he gets into serious debt, he cajoles the old and sick Lingayya to part with his hard-earned savings. As a result, when Lingayya dies, the family is forced to borrow heavily to meet the funeral expenses. After several years, when there is labour trouble at Krishnan's tea factory, Rangan arrives on the scene and begins to incite the workers against their management. In the ensuing skirmish, Rangan is grievously injured and dies before he can be taken to the hospital. After Rangan's death, the feud is forgotten as Krishnan arranges a marriage between his granddaughter Vijaya and Nanjan, Jogi's son. The two warring families are united in marriage but Jogi feels that the price he has paid has been steep, due to the advent of modernisation.

Rangan stands as a character who is representative of the pitfalls of the materialistic outlook that was largely introduced by colonialist capitalism. In earlier times, the Badaga tribe did not know the taste of money; they grew all the food for their needs and bartered the excess for necessities like salt, oil and clothing. The desire to consume exotic foodstuffs, enjoy the cinema and horseraces, and accumulate wealth to raise one's social status were changes that came in with the advent of white men to the Nilgiris. However, it is not as though Krishnan wished the tribe to remain in a 'primitive' state. Through the character of Krishnan, she is able to show the positive effects of modernity and education. While it is true that Jogi loses his lands, his livelihood, and the Badaga traditions that are dear to him, he remains a respected member of the community. Krishnan does acquire Western education and British techniques of tea planting and manufacturing, but he uses his wealth and social status to help others who have not been as fortunate as him. Rangan, who succumbs to the superficial lure of Western ways, is depicted as a man who compromises his community and his integrity. As he is faithful neither to Western culture nor his indigenous roots, Rangan's is the greatest failure. Nevertheless, his life serves as a warning for those who lack the moral fibre to resist the surface attractions of Western cultural mores.

Another major character in the novel is Paru, Jogi's cousin. She is married to Rangan as per the customs of the tribe who are endogamous and practise cross-cousin marriages. Paru shares Jogi's deep love for the land: when her children die of disease, she turns to the land for solace and tends it as she would a child, believing that 'nothing in life gave her as much joy as the land' (Krishnan, 2002, 134). When Jogi's wife dies in childbirth, Paru becomes a foster mother to the child, Nanjan. The child is precocious and does well at school. In an ironic twist, however, the growing prosperity of the area, due to the establishment of the tea plantations and the advent of outside labour, leads to an expansion of the local school.

Krishnan graciously contributes some land to this expansion, as does Jogi, but it is Paru's small plot of land, inherited from her grandfather, that is the most suitably located for the science block. Jogi informs the schoolmaster that the land he is asking for is Paru's and emphasises her deep love for her land. To this, the schoolmaster replies that she will receive handsome compensation. Her retort at being told to part with her land for the greater good of the community conveys her anguish and utter desolation: 'Can you equate money to my land?' (Krishnan, 2002, 185). The strategy used here to displace Paru and Jogi from the land is a classic instance of the appeal for self-sacrifice, claiming that it is for the greater good.

In this context, Michael Cernea's views are pertinent. In his analysis of the environmental and human impact of development-induced displacement, he highlights damaging economic and social costs and their long-enduring negative consequences. Cernea (2011) also focuses on the effects of 'restriction of access' instituted through some development projects (93). He observes that development projects may sometimes cause obstructions in local livelihood activities not just because the land is required for 'right of way', but also for creating, without expropriation, safety zones that limit access to previous local activities. Such a situation is seen in the lives of Jogi and Paru. When their land is partially appropriated for the expansion of the school, this restricts their access to their remaining lands, and as a result they are unable to continue the agricultural work that would make their farm economically viable. This has long-term negative consequences on the family as they are reduced to the status of agricultural labour, dependent on the whims of Jogi's uncle who owns the land at Mookumalai, a hilly region located a short distance away from Jogi's birthplace, Maragathamalai. Eventually, with the construction of the hydro-electric dam at Mookumalai, the uncle also loses his lands as they are acquired for the construction of storage godowns for the project. Due to the total disregard for social equity, a consequence of the cavalier attitude of the colonial government towards those displaced by the dam, those displaced people end up impoverished and worse off.

Jogi and Paru shift to an uncle's farm at Mookumalai, where they are tenant farmers. They are displaced from this location as well, as this land is acquired to construct godowns for the upcoming dam project. Having lost his land at two locations due to various encroachments and having lost his livelihood, his traditions and Nanjan, his son – who becomes a civil engineer – Jogi is rendered a 'subaltern'. David Ludden (2013) uses this term to mean one whose history and culture have been previously ignored. This may be read in relation to the Subaltern Studies movement, a cultural critique of colonialism that was initiated by Ranajit Guha amongst others to focus on histories 'from below': chiefly in accounts of peasant insurgencies, colonial texts, the vernacular resistance movement, communalism, ethnography and related topics. Subaltern Studies is wedded to anthropological history by an insistence on the opposition between 'indigenous' and 'colonial' knowledge. In the narrative of the nation, accounts such as these are elided in elitist histories.

In a character-centric novel such as this, it is interesting to note which character traits may be categorised as environmentally virtuous. Environmental virtues ethics is a relatively new area in moral philosophy that articulates the relationship between environmental virtue and rightful action. Among environmentally conscious individuals, there are some that make for effective environmental exemplars: characters that are recognised as environmental role models. As Ronald Sandler and Philip Cafaro (2005) note: 'by examining the lives of such exemplars of environmental excellence, it is possible to identify particular traits that are constitutive of that excellence' (5). In *When the Kurinji Blooms*, Jogi is one such character, whose life exemplifies an existence lived in harmony with nature. He exhibits traits such as wonder towards nature, perseverance and restraint regarding the use of natural resources. Besides such characteristics, he is compassionate towards all living and non-living entities, he aims at increasing understanding and he displays virtues that are aimed at protecting environmental goods and values, traits that are considered environmentally productive virtues. In Jogi, the author creates an exemplar of environmental virtues whose destiny highlights the slow violence of capitalist developmental strategies. Cederlöf and Sivaramakrishnan (2006) note the appropriation of economic and religious geographies in South Asia as reference points for national aspirations. It is through such ethnographic narratives as *When the Kurinji Blooms* that writers like Krishnan stake their claim to the nation–space of such disenfranchised communities.

Expressions of nationality and nationhood have a long and complicated history in India. Communities and regions have long adopted certain geographies as a reference point or space for the articulation of their national aspirations. Such articulations have justified their version of the nation by locating their origins in the ancient past. By placing these putatively ancient identities in the present, they seek to legitimate their claims to the nation–space. In this quest images have come to play a crucial role. The iconography of flora and fauna characteristic of a region are adopted to redraw the boundaries of nations. This is not merely a recent phenomenon; such rhetoric had been employed since the colonial era when the East India Company moved to take over the forests and hills of the Indian subcontinent. Recent developments have sharpened debates over nature and interrogated the relations between contested natural spaces, place-based collective identities and competing nationalisms in the wake of colonialism in India.

At the level of the state's development initiatives, there are instances where the wilderness and tribal peoples have been introduced to the privileges of modernity. Some historians have seen this as a way of domesticating social forces that create an agenda in terms of 'region' or 'nation' in an attempt to find a space within the political scheme of the nation-state. Therefore, with these multiple communities and varying agendas, aspirations and expressions of nationhood come into conflict. In the last decades of the 20th century, the severity of such conflicts has increased as the gap widens between the territorial, political and economic spaces occupied by these development projects and by local communities. When tribal identities with territorial claims seek to assert their rights to nature within the national space, they come into conflict with metropolitan secular nationalisms that legitimate the nation-state's pre-eminent claim in the contested arena of nature. In this context, *When the Kurinji Blooms* is an ethnographic narrative that articulates the anguish of those displaced by the operation of colonial capital: developmental refugees who are denied the benefits that accrue from these projects. They are doubly disenfranchised, losing their cultural heritage and their ancestral lands as well as any chance of finding an alternative livelihood, as they lack marketable skills and the means to acquire them when they are removed from their accustomed social milieu. In the triumphalist teleology of colonial rhetoric, they are merely 'collateral damage'.

Works cited

Cederlöf, Gunnel (2006). 'The Toda Tiger: Debates on Custom, Utility and Rights in Nature, South India 1820–1843'. In: Cederlöf, Gunnel, and K. Sivaramakrishnan (eds.) *Ecological Nationalisms: Nature, Livelihoods, and Identities in South Asia*. Seattle, WA: University of Washington Press, pp. 65–89.

Cederlöf, Gunnel, and K. Sivaramakrishnan (eds.) (2006). *Ecological Nationalisms: Nature, Livelihoods, and Identities in South Asia*. Seattle, WA: University of Washington Press.

Cernea, Michael (2011). 'Broadening the Definition of "Population Displacement": Geography and Economics in Conservation Policy'. In: Mathur, Hari Mohan (ed.) *Resettling Displaced People*. New Delhi: Routledge, pp. 85–119.

Clifford, James (1986). 'Introduction: Partial Truths'. In: Clifford, James and George E. Marcus (eds.) *Writing Culture: The Poetics and Politics of Ethnography*. Berkeley, CA: University of California Press, pp. 1–26.

Crosby, Alfred W. (2015). *Ecological Imperialism: The Biological Expansion of Europe 900–1900*. Cambridge: Cambridge University Press.

Gadgil, Madhav, and Ramachandra Guha (1995). *Ecology and Equity: The Use and Abuse of Nature in Contemporary India*. New Delhi: Penguin.

Grove, Richard H. (1995). *Green Imperialism: Colonial Expansion, Tropical Island Edens and the Origins of Environmentalism, 1600–1860*. Cambridge: Cambridge University Press.

Guha, Ramachandra and Joan Martinez Alier (1997). *Varieties of Environmentalism: Essays from North and South*. New Delhi: Oxford University Press.

Klingensmith, Daniel (2007). *One Valley and a Thousand: Dams, Nationalism and Development*. New Delhi: Oxford University Press.

Krishnan, Rajam (2002). *When the Kurinji Blooms* (orig. publ. 1962), trans. Uma Narayanan and Prema Seetharam. New Delhi: Orient Longman.

Ludden, David (2013). *Reading Subaltern Studies*. New Delhi: Permanent Black.

Nixon, Rob (2010). 'Unimagined Communities: Developmental Refugees, Megadams and Monumental Modernity'. *New Formations*, 69, 62–80.

Nixon, Rob (2011). *Slow Violence and the Environmentalism of the Poor*. Cambridge, MA: Harvard University Press.

Sandler, Ronald and Philip Cafaro (eds.) (2005). *Environmental Virtue Ethics*. Boulder, CO: Rowman and Littlefield.

7 Material memory and the Partition of India

A narrative interview with Aanchal Malhotra

E. Dawson Varughese

In 2017, in India and elsewhere, the 70 years since Partition were marked in many and various ways. Cultural events, media coverage, diplomatic and transnational programmes all focussed on an event that dramatically changed the course of political and national history. Much of the cultural activity in particular explored people's memories of Partition, with radio and television documentaries interviewing those who had become refugees overnight, asking difficult questions about witnessing and experiencing trauma as well as the struggles to make new lives in new locations. The legacy of Partition was also covered in some detail: from geopolitical legacies to more personal accounts of lost relatives and sometimes, more cheerily, of friendships that had managed to survive divides of all kinds over the years. One aspect of Partition that was less documented was the movement of objects across borders as refugees fled to make new lives elsewhere. Aanchal Malhotra's book *Remnants of a Separation* (2017) is a study of material memory about Partition and thus looks at which objects travelled across borders in bags, suitcases, pockets and hidden under clothes as their owners were forced to leave not only their house but also most of their belongings behind.

E. Dawson Varughese, whose research considers the artistic encoding of societal change within post-millennial India, is in conversation with Malhotra whose recent book has been described as being 'part memoir, part social history' by Shashi Tharoor. It was published by HarperCollins India in 2017, marking the 70th anniversary of Partition. In this interview, Dawson Varughese and Malhotra explore the role that material culture plays in moments of rupture and transition, asking questions about the functional use of 'objects' (for instance, which 'practical' objects do you choose to take with you when you flee?) as well as questions about how personal emotions and memories become embedded (and embodied) within such items. Some time is spent discussing the methodological approaches of *Remnants of a Separation* and in turn, the conversation explores how the 'object' of a material memory research study both leads and gives way to a certain kind of thinking, reminiscing and reinvocation of the past. Varughese invites Malhotra to comment on her own journey researching *Remnants of a Separation*, which began in 2013 at her maternal grandparents'

Material memory and the Partition of India   105

house in New Delhi when a *ghara* (a metallic vessel) and a *gaz* (a yardstick) were brought out from closets to help recount family history. Malhotra writes of this moment as one when the importance of material memory really dawned on her. Given that Malhotra was born into a family affected by Partition, the conversation also explores her own responses to an event that left deep emotional memories for her grandparents. How has Malhotra come to 'remember' Partition and how has *Remnants* as a research project shaped her 'remembering'? Varughese asks how Malhotra approached and engaged with her family's material memory alongside that of other subjects in her research specifically, and how she negotiated the researcher–participant experience. The conversation also considers how Malhotra's experience of living with her grandparents and, importantly, with her grandmother's material memories, shaped the manner in which she approached the topic of Partition and what this experience has afforded her for her own life story.

EDV: Aanchal, the subtitle of your book *Remnants of a Separation* is 'a history of the Partition through material memory' and this is interesting on several levels, not least in that you refer to partition as 'the' partition, accentuating the definitiveness of the act, a sentiment you carry forward when on the inner sleeve of the dust jacket, you refer to an 'Undivided India' and a time before 'the Divide'. Your use of capitals cannot be ignored. And yet this 'definitiveness' of the act of Partition is offset by the variety of both personal memories and the objects that are attached to these memories. I am curious to know how *Remnants* carves out its own sense of 'material memory' and how you see your particular set of case studies (if indeed, they should be described as such) demonstrating the link between material culture and national moments of 'Divide', rupture and transition.

AM: There are several factors that make the Partition of the Indian subcontinent in 1947 a definitive act. Apart from the carving-out of territory, dividing one country into two, perhaps the most important fact is that it is to date the largest mass migration of people in the recorded history of the world. According to a chapter titled 'The State of the World's Refugees' in the UNHCR report of 2009, the official numbers of this migration amount to approximately 14 million displaced and 1 million dead. The Partition of India remains a complex event even today where, despite 70 years having passed, one cannot attribute the events that unravelled in 1947 to a single cause or community, the notion of singular responsibility thereby being absent. One cannot say with certainty that it was the Hindus, Muslims, Sikhs or even the British who were responsible, for ultimately everyone suffered in one way or another. It is all of the above, along with several other factors, that led to this division.

Partition has served as material for a significant amount of research in the areas of politics, sociology, anthropology, psychology and feminism, which have all only recently been classified thematically under the domain of Partition Studies. However, until the publication of my book, no study existed on material culture, memory and refugees, asking about the things – precious or mundane – that people chose to carry with them when they left their homes on either side of the border: things that are not displayed in museums and archives but exist in the personal collections of people's homes and lives.

When I began my work in 2013, the idea of objects seemed bound by utility. The reason for this was that people, upon hearing the focus of my study, wanted to show things that were either monetarily valuable or functionally useful. At the beginning then, I ended up archiving a number of kitchen utensils of varying kinds, I was shown jewellery and other conventionally valuable objects, and documents. But soon, as the field of study grew to encompass a variety of geographic areas, religions, ethnicities, classes and castes, I realised that the range of objects was far greater and not always determined by requirement. Apart from the things one would *need* on the other side, what did people *choose* to take? This choice plays an important role here, for it allows the refugee the luxury to carry something of emotional significance or of familial, cultural, traditional or religious value. The moment my interviewees realised that I wasn't only looking for objects of great and obvious worth, other smaller artefacts were brought out. These ranged from pens, notebooks and books, furniture, engraved cigarette cases and soap dishes, textiles and fabrics, silver and gold *zari* threads sewn onto clothes, theological texts, handwritten documents, letters, trunks, swords, old photographs, and even a 15.5 ft taxidermied crocodile!

What all these objects had in common, apart from the fact that they were 'carried' across, was that they seemed to serve as catalysts for remembrance. The textures of a particular thing, the pattern of another, the frayed edge of a document or the smudged ink of a book almost always held a story and that story was really the crux of this study. Can we use the object to shed light on memories of a home that has now been rendered inaccessible by a national border? Can the object serve as a gentle way of entering into the narrative of an otherwise traumatic past? Can we return with the help of the object, and most importantly, do we want to?

EDV: The chapters are sequenced alphabetically and are clearly demarcated, as each one is prefaced by a 'title page' upon which your own photograph of the object (or person) at the centre of the 'memory' is printed. It is mainly the case that the chapter title speaks directly of the object of memory as we see in 'The Pearls of Azra Haq', 'The Photographs of Nazeer Adhami', and 'The Assorted Curios of Prof. Sat Pal Kohli'. I'm curious as to the choice behind foregrounding the image of the 'material memory' on this title page which is in contrast with the unhurried, slow revelation of the nature of the memory, demonstrated through your ethnographic and thus often poetic description of the context and memory itself.

AM: The image, I felt, was a necessity in the book. While speaking about the texture, form, colour and age of an object, it is necessary to be able to see it. And so each chapter's title page begins with the image of the object being discussed.

Material memory and the Partition of India 107

Figure 7.1 'The Pearls of Azra Haq' © Aanchal Malhotra.

The page is turned and only then does the narrative begin. The aim of each account is to understand a life before and after Partition, demonstrated through memory and conversation triggered by the object(s).

Each interview lasted hours, where the object wasn't always brought out immediately, even though the interviewee knew that was to be the focus of our conversation. However, we must acknowledge that Partition is not just about what remained or what was lost, it is also about the years and months that led up to it, and those which were endured by refugees right after. It wasn't immediate; it was also unhurried and gradual and it built up, both politically and socially, to what we now know as the demarcating Radcliffe Line.

Most importantly, memory in itself, or the remembrance of certain memories and the past, is not always chronological. These interviews were not recorded in chronological fashion, starting from childhood to Partition, for people remember things sporadically. Therefore, a slow, eventual narrative is what emerged, presenting almost always an exact reproduction of our conversation as well. Furthermore, archiving the minutiae of movement, the change in one's facial features, the lilting of voice that accompanied the narration of the object's history – a gasp, a sigh, the soft stroke of a finger on its surface, even a gesture of nonchalance and dismissal – became my main aim.

These stories strive to appreciate the object in its totality, not as something that blends into the landscape of the past but as a primary character around which the entire landscape is arranged, and so putting it into the context of that landscape – whether it be of the present day or 70 years ago – became equally important.

EDV: How did you come to talk to the people who feature in your book? How did you make contact with them initially?

AM: I would like to say that I had a structured model in mind to contact people but really the project grew as sporadically and organically as the initial idea. It is not difficult to locate refugees, especially in New Delhi, where I live, but as I found out within the first few months of my field research, finding objects was a laborious task. At the beginning, my family became my main mode of foraging; word of mouth became a familiar means and sure enough, slowly and gradually, I began to visit people who shared with me objects and memories from across the border. My aunt, during her daily walks in New Delhi's Defence Colony, would fearlessly approach older men and women from the neighbourhood, armed with questions about their potential memorabilia. My parents, who run Bahrisons Booksellers in New Delhi, would do the same when they learned of a customer's connection to the Partition in any way.

Eventually, the project grew large enough that people began contacting me themselves. I received messages through friends, through email, and even through social media. One thing I would like to emphasise here is the role of social media in the expansion of areas of research for this work. When I began interviewing people in 2013, our conversations revealed things about Indian history that I had never read about in books or other texts. These were obviously people's personal stories, but they offered versions of the same event about which knowledge had been limited and channelled for me through the state narrative published in our school and college history textbooks in India. Despite all four of my grandparents having migrated from across the border, I had never really been interested in stories of Partition until I began this work. The exposure that I had to the variety of narratives was so immense and altering that I began sharing snippets of these conversations on a blog, *The Hiatus Project*, and on Instagram, an essentially visual online medium. Very soon, these social media outlets became very popular and the stories of people and objects seemed relatable to many. Apart from comments and questions, what poured in were requests, often from third- or fourth-generation descendants of Partition-affected families, for me to come to their homes and record their personal and material histories. The internet, a democratic medium which is delightfully borderless, also allowed for people of different ethnicities and nationalities (say, an Indian, a Pakistani, and a Bangladeshi), who would otherwise be limited by national frontiers, to interact with one another about a particular story or object on my blog, which they had each perhaps seen being used in their respective houses.

Sometimes interviews also happened as a result of a chance encounter with the elderly at weddings, family lunches or dinners, on flights, train rides and even public transport. In the quest to search for interesting and unique objects (and their subsequent narratives), I was looking to exhaust every possible method to obtain information. However, it is important to stress that in the end, word of mouth played a significant role, where I was often given the contacts of someone or someone's grandparents through a family member, friend, acquaintance or work colleague. But even then, the degrees of removal could sometimes be very vast. For example, the chapter, 'A Conversation of Eroded Memory: The Identification Certificates of Sunil Chandra Sanyal', is about Sanyal, a man who lives in Kolkata: the father of the music teacher of my father's third cousin living in Bangalore. Another instance, the chapter, 'Hereditary Keepers of the Raj: The Enduring Memories of John Grigor Taylor', is written as a result of a chance conversation I once had during a meeting with Taylor's daughter, Imogen Taylor, publisher of Headline Books UK. She happened to mention that her English father was born and raised in British India and continued to have strong ties with the Indian subcontinent and the Hindustani language.

Lastly, the research could not, of course, be limited to people who simply moved across to India from what became Pakistan. It also had to encompass the objects and experiences of those who chose to or were forced to migrate to Pakistan. The Citizens Archive of Pakistan initially facilitated my research in Pakistan where I worked for a month in 2014 as a short-term researcher. However, after spending significant time there, I did make several contacts who have helped me on subsequent trips.

EDV: In 'The Hopeful Heart of Nazmuddin Khan', there is no memento, no object of a time gone by. He talks of the land itself as a site of remembrance wherein the bodies of Muslims are buried, just as the ashes of Hindus run in the great rivers, and in this act, the Muslim *becomes* Hindustan as his remains are subsumed into the 'nation'. In 'The *hamam-dasta* of Savitri Mirchandani', the *hamam-dasta* (or pestle and mortar) that travels with her across the Arabian Sea is slipped, unbeknown to Savitri, into the suitcase by an *ayah*. Leaving Sindh behind with only a suitcase and her two children, Savitri discovers the *hamam-dasta* only as she unpacks her belongings in her new 'home', India. Both these vignettes of memory surely challenge some of the ideas that began this enquiry since in the former, there is no 'object' and in the latter, the object was not 'chosen' to be carried in the suitcase. Could you say how your own ideas of material memory and Partition were changed and shaped by the variety of people you met and objects you encountered?

AM: Sometimes I think that I have spent too much time surrounded by old objects to be able to view situations independent of that lens. With Nazmuddin Khan, the non-presence of an object left me feeling sort of aimless during our interview. As he was speaking, I kept thinking to myself, 'But what will I archive? What is my subject here if there is no object?' But very soon that aimlessness

110 E. Dawson Varughese

Figure 7.2 'Nazmuddin Khan seated outside his home in Hauz Rani, New Delhi, 2014'
© Aanchal Malhotra.

transformed into me feeling rather small and insignificant in the light of what he had experienced: mass murder and ethnic cleansing in the Hauz Rani area of New Delhi, where he resided in 1947. I included his story, for it made me realise that the nature of the object is not limited to the physical and that, because this study was mine alone, the nature of the object could transform into one that was, say, intangible, like the memory and values of being Hindustani, which – as he was trying to make me understand – surpassed all communal categorisation.

For Savitri Mirchandani, the presence of the *hamam-dasta* was known to her only after she arrived in India. However, because I had been introduced to the object before and the story of how it was carried came much later in our conversation, the absence of the object from her narrative was far less impactful. Perhaps this was coupled with the fact that as a person, Mirchandani is not very emotional, and so the past was narrated in a rather detached tone.

It's important to make note here of the vignette of Aquila Ahsan from Lahore, who speaks briefly about the bump on her head that she received from falling down the stairs while fleeing from a pack of monkeys in Aligarh: that bump is the only physical memento that remains with her of her lost India. There are also stories of objects that no longer remain, like the *chadar* (or veil) of Bua, a woman who used to come to Zehra Nasim Haque's home to cook. The story is narrated by Haque. In the book, I write:

> She [Haque] recalls that Bua had once told her [Haque's] mother that at the time of Partition she had been a young woman, fleeing from the riots on a train from Delhi to Lahore. Somewhere midway, rioters entered the carriages

Material memory and the Partition of India 111

and killed many people, including her husband, who was even thrown off the train. Jumping after him, Bua sat by his corpse as his blood oozed out and on to the ground around him. Using her *chadar*, she soaked up as much of his blood as she could. Having barely been married for a few years, child on the way, she collected as much as she could of her husband and, with a heavy heart, asked the train conductor to bury him where he lay. Taking his word as a promise, she made her way all alone to Lahore across the new border. There, without home or bearings, she went to a graveyard and had the blood-soaked *chadar* buried to mark the grave of her late husband. When their child was born, she took him there, week after week, year after year, to be acquainted with the father he never knew. "Bua never married again," Zehra said, "and lived in Lahore with her children, grandchildren and a wound in her heart till she passed."

When I heard this story from Haque in Karachi, I had wished deeply to be able to see the blood-soaked *chadar* or even speak to Bua about this particular incident in her life. Since she had passed on a few years before, this was not possible. But the sheer impact that the story had on Haque herself as she narrated it to me, teary-eyed – despite it not being a story about her own family – as well as the sheer poetic gesture of a widowed woman burying whatever little she could carry of her husband across the border where they'd hoped to begin their life, made it essential for this particular story to be included in the book. And so, we see here that as the years of living with this research have progressed, the conventional boundaries of the 'object' have certainly softened to include the intangible and the testimonial as well as the invisible.

EDV: Your book has been described as an oral history, a study of material cultures and as social ethnography and it has been praised for its thorough and wide-ranging research. As both a trained (art) historian and a trained artist, how was the approach to the fieldwork shaped by these areas of enquiry and practice?

AM: I have often thought about this, and always come to the conclusion that it is because of my training in the fine arts (traditional printmaking and art history) that this project has become as immersive as it is. During each interview, though I'd always record the conversation, I'd also be taking notes and these notes were often on movements, gestures, the lilting of voice, the change in light, the colours of someone's clothes, the crinkle of a brow, and other minutiae. I would also draw small sketches of people and their surroundings as much as I could. And so perhaps the greatest gift I could have brought as an artist to a work of this nature is the gift of observation.

Each chapter thus also comes together not just from the primary interviews or the secondary research, but really, from my time as a practising artist and my experiences of synaesthesia. This book is driven by the senses, it is sensory above anything else – it includes touch, feel, smell, sight, sound, memory. The senses are situated at the forefront of all methods of remembrance. It is important to view this work as born from fine art and then evolving into literature. Images here have morphed into language. The soft folds of a shawl and the sharp edges of an old pocketknife have reshaped themselves to become the soft 's's and sharp 'f's you see printed on the page before you. The final work, *Remnants of a Separation*, has thus emerged as a collaboration between words and images: the conceptual, the factual, the historical and the visual.

Moreover, I have transformed from a person who makes things – an artist – to a person who collects things. I have become a collector of objects and their associated memories, an antiquarian or an archivist of sorts. I have found solace in textures, crevasses, cracks, folds and polish. They have become familiar attributes of an even more familiar landscape, and I have learnt to cultivate their physicality with some ease.

EDV: How has the 'object' of a material memory led and given way to a certain kind of thinking, reminiscing and reinvocation of the past? How central was the haptic experience of holding and feeling the object in each of the case studies and how did this act feed into the way in which you documented your work?

AM: The object is just an object until it is impregnated with memory. The physical contours of something aged don't evoke anything until they are given importance and situated within someone's recollections of a time and place. In this regard, the holding, feeling, caressing and talking about the object was imperative, for an object could languish at the back of a drawer or in a locker for decades without its rightful importance bestowed upon it as an ambassador of an incredible journey across a contentious border. '*Kuch nahi laaye the.* We brought nothing. We came with nothing,' was easily the first response I got from whoever

Figure 7.3 'Aanchal Malhotra interviewing Uma Sondhi Ahmad at her home in Kolkata, 2018' © Karuna Ezara Parikh.

Material memory and the Partition of India 113

I asked about their belongings from 1947. But then things would eventually crawl out of the backs of closets, suitcases and trunks, sheathed in dust and infused with dormant memories.

During the course of working with these objects, certain questions also emerged in my mind about the way we deal with material culture, particularly in the subcontinent and particularly if the 'thing' is not something which is obviously of monetary value, but exceedingly mundane like a utensil or a book. I wanted to know what it felt like to hold in one's hands a tangible part of one's history, a history which now belonged on the other side of the border. How did one approach it? Was it a prized possession or something too mundane to be considered of value? Was it allowed the luxury of touch and feel and smell, the sensual caress of fingers and skin, or was it to remain elusive in its tactility, situated behind glass, stored safely at the back of a closet? Moreover, what did this object convey to its owner? Was its importance immediately recognised, did it demand an audience, was the story of its serendipitous survival known and celebrated or abandoned and forgotten? Could it be used as a guide for recollection, a propagator of the past?

And so, it was essential that the object be brought out and discussed and passed around and scrutinised during our conversation. People often even discovered spots or scratches, as in the case of Preet Singh and the shawl she had been given from her mother as they fled from Quetta to Mussourie; people stumbled upon text and inscriptions they'd never seen before, as in the case of Uma Sondhi Ahmad and the trunk belonging to her father, the director of the Geological Survey of India; and in this way, the object sometimes gained new meaning, both for the people it belonged to as well as for the purposes of my study.

EDV: Relatedly, how was the experience of holding *other people's* memories different from the moment in 2013 when at your maternal grandparents' house in New Delhi, a *ghara* and a *gaz* were brought out from closets to help recount family history? Given your own closeness to a legacy of Partition, how did you engage with family material memory alongside the material memory of others? My feeling is that this negotiation lies at the heart of a researcher–participant experience and I wonder when this first came up for you and how you allowed (or didn't allow) this facet of the enquiry to be part of the journey?

AM: To answer the first part of the question, I would like to draw attention to the chapter, 'The Dialect of Stitches and Secrets: The Bagh of Hansla Chowdhary'. In a suburb of New Delhi, I was shown a traditional Punjabi textile called a *bagh* – larger in size than a shawl or scarf – and hand-stitched by Sardarni Sundar Kaur Sabharwal, the great-grandmother of Hansla Chowdhary and subsequently presented to Chowdhary's grandmother, Gobind Kaur. The embroidery done on coarse, very warm *khaddar* fabric is known as *phulkari*, which means flower work, *phul* meaning 'flower' and *kari* meaning 'craft' in Punjabi. The earliest mention of the word *phulkari* can be found in the love story of Heer–Ranjha, written by Waris Shah, where Heer wears many outfits with such embroidery. It depicts the blossoming of flowers, the lightness, the spring. The Punjabi word *bagh* itself translates to 'garden'.

114 E. Dawson Varughese

Figure 7.4 'The Dialect of Stitches and Secrets: The *Bagh* of Hansla Chowdhary'
© Aanchal Malhotra.

Throughout our conversation, Chowdhary explained to me how traditional *phulkari* was done only by the women of a family, village or clan, in preparation for a celebration: say, a girl's wedding or her baby shower. It can be considered a means of socialising, for when these women got together, they would talk and share cups of *chai* and stitch the fabric. Special songs were sung – songs of marriage, the solemn sadness of having to part with one's daughter, or songs of happiness at the birth of children, the flowering of a womb – and the energy from these would subliminally flow into the work. *Phulkari* became a language of the women, decorative and beautiful, and every stitch appeared on the fabric as a rendition of that private dialect.

This *bagh* had been passed down, as I mentioned, from Chowdhary's great-grandmother, to her grandmother, and then to her, and clearly, being over 100 years old, it held great familial significance and value. It had been carried by Gobind Kaur when she migrated from Rawalpindi to Delhi during the Partition, when unable to pack it in to her sparse luggage or bear to leave it behind, she was forced to wear it in the unbearable August heat. After our conversation was over and I was photographing the *bagh*, Chowdhary picked it up from the sofa where it lay and placed it on my shoulders to show me how it usually would have been worn. I remember that moment when, instinctively, I had drawn my breath in and had sat up straighter, wanting my posture to be worth the beauty and fragility of the treasured piece. But even then, something didn't feel quite right. Beautiful though it was, on my shoulders it sat awkwardly and out of place, devoid of its genealogy and history. The strangest feeling crept over me as if I was privy to a secret that didn't belong to me. I felt like a trespasser on a family's ancestry. And so, slowly and carefully, I removed it and placed it on the shoulder of its rightful owner. This feeling occurred many times, when I felt – not only with the object, but also just the nature of vulnerable memory that was being divulged to me – as though I was an intruder. Time and again, I was entering a world that was not mine, and sometimes, through my questions about the past and its moments of trauma, I was causing great pain, when all forms of such pain had been seemingly long forgotten, sometimes on purpose and sometimes due to age.

As I reflect back over these last five years on how large the nascent idea I once had has become, I can't help but notice how much I, too, have changed. The memories of others have affected me in ways I find hard to put down in words. Their voices, their language, their sorrow and their lament have settled into me; I have inherited so many people's accounts that they feel almost like my own. I have a responsibility towards them: to listen, to extract, to analyse, to share and to learn from the horrors they experienced in the hope that no one ever experiences them again. The lives of others have become inextricably linked with my own in a way that makes them feel no different than family. This family comprises grandmothers, grandfathers, uncles and aunts; Punjabi, Bengali, Sindhi, Kashmiri, Dogra, Rajasthani, Gujarati; Hindus, Muslims, Sikhs, Parsis, Christians, Buddhists; Indians, Pakistanis, Bangladeshis, and many others who are helping to reconstruct the history of this great Partition through their personal stories, demonstrating with each narrative that the individual voice matters.

As for the second part of the question: I think engaging with family history can be both complex and fascinating. When I chanced upon the objects belonging to both sides of my family, whether they were the *ghara* and *gaz*, or even the pocketknife, old photos, *maang-tikka* or utensils, I could never have imagined the expanse of storytelling such objects would encompass. Perhaps the most important and also the most difficult thing was to view personal family history through the lens of a researcher and archivist, to treat it empirically (insofar as memory can be treated) rather than emotionally. Thus the chapters on my family, though they were written quite early on in, were edited and reworked at the very end.

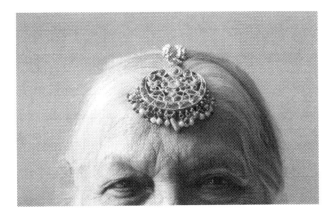

Figure 7.5 'Stones from My Soil: The *Maang-Tikka* of Bhag Malhotra'
© Aanchal Malhotra.

I must also mention that in the course of writing the book, my paternal grandfather, Balraj Bahri, died and his chapter perhaps tormented me the most. I remember, I stuck his photograph on the wall of my study and whenever I'd listen to his audio recordings, I'd speak to the photograph. There was so much about him that I didn't know, so much about his emotional psyche as a refugee in the years after the Partition, which had been buried under the veneer of successful entrepreneurship. I was piecing together a life of someone I knew so intimately, yet somehow didn't know at all, after he had passed. And though the story was only about the utensils his mother carried, the same utensils which had been used to cook food for the family in refugee camps and drink water from on crowded train stations in August 1947, in the interview the only things my grandfather had volunteered to speak about were the beautiful orchards and fruit trees they left behind in Malakwal (present-day West Punjab, Pakistan). Any sense of longing or remorse for leaving 'home' behind had to be brought out by me by puncturing through the heart of his narrative and asking unaskable questions. He conceded eventually, but the process had been anything but easy for us both. And so, it is safe to say that I found it difficult to enter and re-enter into memories that were very much a part of me and my history, but I had known so little about prior to this work. That being said, the desire to do justice to them was far greater.

8 Thinking gender in 21st-century India
Reflections on *Drawing the Line: Indian Women Fight Back*

Sukeshi Kamra

'This is a wonderful time to be a feminist with greedy eyes', Nisha Susan writes more than once in her Introduction to *Drawing the Line: Indian Women Fight Back* (2015), a collection of graphic narratives by Indian women, edited by Priya Kurian, Larissa Bertonasco and Ludmilla Bartscht. The reasons she offers for believing this to be the case conjure up a rich landscape of women's voices and an irreducible variety of subjects and approaches:

> You could start the morning with a quick dip into Tatsuya Ishida's wonderful, long-running web-comic, *Sinfest*. It might be any one of Ishida's gem-like strips: perhaps the ever-popular one in which, over four panels, the protagonist sits at her laptop typing a Feminist Utopia Fantasy Story which, in its entirety, reads: "It was midnight. Amanda felt like going for a walk. So she did. The End" ... You could take a gentle stroll through carefully curated photo essays about a pair of Dutch trans teenagers. Or read a graphic novel about the rich and turbulent life of Cuban-American artist Ana Mendieta or visual journalism about the life of a young Ethiopian woman employed by an oppressive Saudi household. You can be awed by the reckless gallantry of a viral video in which a young Iranian woman records herself dancing to Little Mix, her face uncovered, inside a subway train in Tehran. Or watch a delightful animation celebrating birth control with dancing condoms.
>
> (Susan, 2015, 2)

The history, however, which served as the genesis of a week-long workshop in New Delhi in 2014 – of which the collection is the end product or its trace (depending on one's perspective) – is the very sobering reality that faces Indian women in 21st-century India. Here are the very first few sentences of the Introduction:

> On December 16, 2012, a young physiotherapy student was gang-raped and brutally beaten in a bus in Delhi. A little over a week later, she died. The uproar this terrifying news caused has never quite died down. Ever since, the debate around sexual violence in India has stayed heated and frequently

118 *Sukeshi Kamra*

infuriating. It has had its usual share of victim-blaming, sensationalising, cuckoo politicians blaming rape on everything from chowmein to mobile phones.

(Susan, 2015, 1)

The list of deeply disturbing reactions to the savage gang rape of Jyoti Singh on the night of 16 December 2012, dredged up by Susan (2015, 1) as she recalls this horrific moment, does not end there. '[P]aranoia about stranger rape', 'paralysing lists of instructions to women on how to be safe', and 'demands that the rapists be hanged or chemically castrated' are among the effects Susan lists. At the most global of levels, both geographically and ideationally, the event was claimed as evidence that 'rape is an Indian problem, a "Third World" problem' (Susan, 2015, 1). That is to say, the event was assimilated to embedded stereotypes by which the global North continues to lay (exclusive) claim to modernity.

The history the Introduction sets up as *the* intertext of the collection, the classically uncanny rupture of 16 December 2012, encourages us to approach *Drawing the Line* as a work of witnessing. The collection is best described as a situated literary collaboration of visual storytelling that speaks to a very specific difficult moment in India's recent past. As such, it promotes the graphic narrative as the genre through which to relate stories of the violence that hide in plain sight in 21st-century India. In so doing, the collection is a poignant comment on the increasing gap between public recall of/engagement with histories of violence on the one hand – mediated as these are in large part by legal, political and sensational media stories – and a reality subject to wilful blindness and neglect. Furthermore, witnessing the 21st-century contemporary moment as it is unfolding in India seems inevitably charged with the notion of milestones by which 1947, the year of India's hard-won independence from Britain, remains in the forefront of the national imagination. Most recently, this view of 'progress' informed Ramachandra Guha's important speech delivered at the 2017 Kerala Literary Festival. Titled 'India at 70: A Historian's Report Card', Guha posed the following simple but profound question: 'How have we done?' (Guha, 2017). The same view, which marks 1947 as the originary moment of 'Indian national time', is discernible in the deep sense of disappointment within graphic narratives that bear witness to the extraordinary in the everyday occurrence of gender, caste and communal violence and indeed in an introduction such as Susan's.

What does witnessing mean and look like? In Susan's reading of the graphic narratives of *Drawing the Line*, witnessing has a different feel to it than one might expect. She says of the collection that 'adapting swiftly to this abundance of lemons, young and older feminists in India have made lemonade' (Susan, 2015, 1). Clearly, witnessing encompasses a refusal to be overwhelmed by the devastation and shock of December 2012 and, judging by Susan's dependence on figurative language, it is indirect rather than direct. (Indeed, only one of the graphic narratives engages directly with the December 2012 event.) One might very well ask: what is the reality conjured up by the term 'lemonade'? In one answer, it is a painstaking re-inking of boundaries that faded in the face of the violent rupture represented by the brutal gang-attack and rape of Jyoti Singh and the media frenzy that followed. Once again, in Susan's words,

> [T]hey [feminists] have used the momentum to broaden the conversations beyond the terror of stranger rape – to talk about work, pay, love, marriage, disability, caste, sex and everyday sexism. These conversations have looped into equally heated feminist debates and interventions around the world.
>
> (Susan, 2015, 1)

We may read in this a statement of refusal to surrender the right of representation, debate and definition to the alarming world of (sensational) media. At a profound level, the collection is nothing if not informed by a desire to disengage the kind of spectatorship witnessed in the media coverage of the event.

There is another equally important answer, which is, more properly speaking, a set of considerations that closely aligns with a figurative engagement of the past. It is an answer we encounter in a different moment of the Introduction, where Susan draws attention to the title of the collection:

> [It] was inspired by Kaveri Gopalakrishnan's brilliant story "Basic Space" in which, in a series of vignettes of urban life and with the lightest of touches, the artist encourages the reader to give up on the paranoia of a post-December 16 India and embrace our messy, chaotic world again.
>
> (Susan, 2015, 3)

'Messy' and 'chaotic' counter terms that seek to demarcate the terrain of Indian feminism:[1] the terms gesture in the direction of meaning rather than claiming to encompass it. It is metaphor that also provides us with Susan's view of the artistic method she perceives to be in place in the graphic narratives of the collection: 'lightest of touches' describes history well engaged, in Susan's view. The painterly phrase takes in 'The Walk', Deepani Seth's story of a woman trolling through scenes of a quintessentially 21st-century Indian town while lazily ruminating on the bric-à-brac of her world at one end; and at the other, Vidyun Sabhaney's story, 'Broken Lines', of a woman confronted with a devastatingly uncanny moment, when the boundaries separating fiction from history are breached, leaving the narrator bewildered about genres of experience.

Laying claim to the figurative as a way of speaking an otherwise unspeakable history, to which Susan's evocative statements on the graphic stories of the collection draw attention, is an important part of the design of the 2014 workshop. Allusive terms ('messy', 'chaotic', 'lightest of touches'), which map imperfectly onto the shocking rupture of an event such as the gang rape of Jyoti Singh, remind us of the gap between complex histories of violence and their meaningful (as opposed to sensational) representation. In the graphic narratives, I would suggest, the same gap is apparent in the divide between a distinct, interpretable world, which each text presents, and women's engaging with it, which does not lend itself as easily to interpretation. Some graphic artists draw attention to this fact in the prefatory blurb they write when they comment on the value they place on open-ended stories.[2] The graphic narratives themselves suggest that what is compassed in the word 'open-endedness' is ambiguity (the condition of) precarity, contradiction, ambivalence and contingency.

What is meant by the 'lightest of touches', the other metaphorical phrase by which the stories are framed in the Introduction, is indicated in the brief blurbs provided by individual graphic storytellers on their art and its relationship to the history it engages. For instance, Diti Mistry, author of 'Bombay Local', writes in the blurb at the foot of the title page of her story that 'hearing stories about Mumbai and coming face to face with the city turned out to be very different. I was lost, and was not sure if I ever wanted to be part of it' (Kurian, Bertonasco, and Bartscht, 2015, n.p.).[3] This casual biographical titbit claims the right to remind us of the small encounters and negotiations as well as shifts in perception with which the everyday is filled, presumably in the face of heavy history. Indeed, 'Bombay Local', set in the women's compartment of a 'local' (suburban) train, expands the micro so that it forms the horizon of the narrative. Identifying herself as an outsider to the world of Mumbai, the narrator's relating of the shift in perception that takes place while on the train – from suspicion of the women in the compartment to a sense of belonging with them – is the story the narrative relates. In another narrative, entitled 'Someday', the graphic artist Samidha Gunjal addresses the form of sexual harassment normalised in India as 'eve-teasing'. The prefatory blurb explains:

> This is a story about one day, a day unlike any other. The girl in my story has to deal with what is euphemistically called "eve-teasing" but in that moment she finds her strength. Her anger takes over and her emotions explode – she becomes Kali![4]

While it is easy to accept that the theme of 'Bombay Local' merits a light touch, juxtaposing sexual objectification and harassment with the phrase 'lightest of touches' may be difficult to accept and may appear inappropriate. It is precisely this disjuncture, however, that makes the heavier stories in the collection intriguing for their revelation of an approach to the writing of gendered history, one that avoids monumentalising the tragic. The story told in Gunjal's 'Someday', which is better described as a visual exploding of a typical 'eve-teasing' incident, makes its point about the willed misrecognition of sexual harassment as 'teasing' by lightly flipping typical scenes of fear and victimisation faced by Indian women every day and harnessing the image of Kali to do so. The last page of the story has a single image in the centre – a figure drawn in black – surrounded by the white space of the page. The terrified woman of the initial moments of an encounter with 'eve-teasing' men is transformed: she sits, nude, with a lit cigarette in one hand while holding a steaming mug of tea or coffee in another. A third arm extends to her full head of open tresses, while a fourth is in her lap. She is winking and smiling. We are, that is, asked to accept the juxtaposition of this everyday performance of sexism with its storying in ways that link recuperation of this very type of story with practical action on the one hand, thus denying any acquiescence to or tolerance of this pervasive form of harassment, and humour on the other. Here it is a humour generated by the mapping of the everyday woman and occurrence onto the mythologically powerful and iconoclastic Kali, updating the latter to suit the 21st century. In 'Basic Space', Gopalakrishnan writes of the inspiration for the compendium of stories that make up her graphic narrative:

> It was a hot summer afternoon in Delhi that led to a whole day of these conversations with fifteen different women, of various age groups and backgrounds. These, in turn, inspired the questioning, sometimes painfully funny, too-serious mini-comics in "Basic Space".

As Gopalakrishnan's employment of an oxymoron ('painfully funny') indicates, she hopes to capture or indeed produce storytelling at the thin edge where painful and funny are indistinguishable.

By reflecting on the Introduction to *Drawing the Line* and drawing attention to the brief prefatory blurbs that front narratives, I have shown that they are as much a place to explore the subject of gendered India in the 21st century, as are the graphic narratives themselves. In what follows, I look at the ways in which space – public, private, interior/psychological, emotional – is structured in particular graphic narratives to describe the irreducibly gendered world of contemporary India, and draw out the ways in which women characters are shown inhabiting, struggling with, shaping or reshaping, reflecting on and making meaning of the world depicted in the text.

In 'Mumbai Local', the world in the text is the teeming metropolis of Mumbai, a powerful metonymy of which is the iconic Mumbai local train. In the women's compartment, which is the world in the text, the city as shared space is as much a focus as is the slim plot of a shift in perception undergone by the narrator during the journey. Space is rendered dynamic and heterogeneous in multiple frames filled to the brim with line drawings of strangers competing for space, while others, in the midst of the mayhem, calmly conduct daily activities: a woman praying on a mat, another chopping vegetables on a board, and the like. The story – of the narrator, whose discovery of an insect in her clothing is met with a spontaneous rallying of the women in the compartment, who provide assistance as she attempts to remove the insect – more than shares the stage with the chaotic and crammed world which the text celebrates. It is not difficult to see that via the spatial and the visual, 'Bombay Local' raises a theme, that of unknowns, their associated danger, and its opposite, security. Thus the graphic story moves towards a minor epiphanic moment – the ephemeral, yet perfect companionship/safety that creeps up on the narrator unawares.

Security – as a line drawn in the sand when it comes to Indian women's reality – is visible in the graphic rendition of space in stories that focus on the familial home. 'The Photo' by Reshu Singh declares its concern with the normatively patriarchal Indian home in the very first page where the narrator is caught in the portrait-pose of the South Asian genre of 'the marriage photo'. Here domestic space holds dangers associated with norms, vocabularies and constraints. It is a space in which we see norms flexible enough to encompass a range of women, differentiated by age. Thus a gendered domestic space, the narrative shows, is far from monolithic. It is differently experienced by young women of marriageable age through the policing of the marketable female body, the teenage girl, the mother, and the grandmother. The latter's stories, and those of the protagonist's younger sister, lurk somewhere behind the story of the young protagonist. The latter's refusal to assent to the family's claim to her future – a fact that her portrait-sitting signifies – takes centre stage. Nonetheless, these women, and the story of their lives, are far from invisible. In another take on domestic space, Harini Kanan's 'That's Not Fair', it is the maternal womb that pinpoints the prefiguring of constraining spaces which India's women must navigate. The image of the maternal womb is, of course, profoundly metonymic of the shameful history of female foeticide in India. In Kanan's narrative, the womb is associated with the less extreme but equally devastating history of threat with which Indian women are faced in the world of the everyday. Here the story told is of the disfiguration associated with the attempt to alter pigmentation: the unborn girl-narrator struggles against her mother's desperate attempt to ensure the child she is carrying is lighter-skinned than she is in the only way that she, the unborn child, can: verbally.

In Priyanka Kumar's 'Ever After', the mundane world of domesticity – which it offers as the given and as a reality defined by lack – is disavowed via ambiguous images of thrilling strangeness, which threaten to erupt and make the space of the mundane unpredictable. In one particularly striking panel, the woman locks into an ecstatic embrace with a sexually powerful monster of a popular television drama series that comes to life. In succeeding panels she is shown poised on the windowsill of her house; entranced by a vision of a monster reflected in her tea; being spoken to by a group of mini-monsters that burst out of a suitcase, presumably one of the two suitcases that, in previous panels, lie under her bed, packed; and, in the final panel, she is missing from an open nocturnal landscape punctured only by an empty open suitcase and a flag on a pole planted in a rocky earth boundaried by a fence. As with some of the background characters in the other stories – for instance, the mother and grandmother in Singh's 'The Photo' and the mother-to-be in Kanan's 'That's Not Fair', the danger represented here, within the domestic arena, is of a complete evacuation of the very notion of women's agency, here most powerfully imagined as a life of entrapment in and by defined roles.

Stories that opt for public spaces and/or traverse boundaries separating public from private/familial are informed by the many shades that the subject of personal security has in a gendered India, including the forms of interrogation of the safety/danger paradigm by which patriarchal control is effected (Priyanka Kumar's 'Ever After' is an example). 'The Walk' by Deepani Seth, the only bilingual graphic story of the collection (Hindi and English), sketches the many everyday spaces a woman inhabits and traverses over the course of a typical day in her life within a known world. The first space to be introduced is the workplace, here a 'beauty salon', where the woman of the story finds herself a confidante to her customers and their sometimes complicated lives: one is about to be married and has yet to inform her boyfriend of this fact. The panels periodically surround the central character with text, which frames the otherwise ambiguous world of image by which the narrative relates her everyday life. The first panel abuts an image of the woman engaged in work. She silently ruminates, 'I sometimes think about how we seek – and often find – secret places in the world, places where we can hide and, hidden thus, reveal ourselves, or parts of ourselves, or become someone else entirely.' The second space to be introduced – her home – is as filled with silence and absences as the first is with stories and internal reflections. There is little conversation between the woman and her husband and we glean that the home is filled with silence and marked by separation. Hence the only conversation that takes place is of the husband informing her that he has to be away for a few days for work reasons. Suitcases on a shelf feature prominently here, too, in multiple panels. What makes the domestic space that much more ambiguous is the noticeable absence of captioned thought, which would have provided an authoritative view.

At the same time, the narrative does not come to a halt with the scene of domestic discomfort. It moves seamlessly to another scene, where the woman is out in the neighbourhood. She interacts with a vegetable seller, passes by people conversing with one another while waiting in line in front of a cinema theatre ticket-window; and, finally, against the backdrop of a night sky, she absent-mindedly picks up an idle comment made by a man having tea with his friends at a tea-stall, 'the moon is alone tonight', and completes it with her own: 'suspended in a quiet comfortable blankness [one panel] that holds within it several unheard stories [another panel] keeping them [another panel] even as the owners and creators of those stories come and go, like travellers, like seasonal nomads moving between temporal spaces' [several panels later]. Seth, who describes herself as a designer, researcher, and illustrator, says of the genesis of the story: '[It] started as a piece of nonfiction, based on a day spent with a woman in a small town in eastern India. It was just supposed to be a telling of a part of her day, which could have been any among the several everydays of her life.' It turned into something more, as she began the process of writing and illustrating. She recalls: 'It became about a woman, in any place, with or without a job, with a home or without one, walking across a city that could have been any city anywhere.' The 'more' seems to collapse distinctions by which the everyday – with its small conversations, activities, disappointments and joys – is presumed to be banal; it seems also to want to question the absolute value placed on individuality (Seth finds the encounter allows her to consider the intertwining of the individual figure, individual day, and individual city with the generic and vice versa).

At the other end of the spectrum, Gunjal's 'Someday' traces the movements of a modern young woman (signs of 'modernity' include cigarette smoking) from the shower (followed by a panel of two towelled women) to the streets where she is subjected to sexual harassment. The transformation of this space by her transformation into a Kali-like figure, suggesting justified and positive anger, gives the story its 'turn': space and history are transformed in and by this one act which is dramatised as a fleeing-away of the same men who had indulged in sexual harassment. The graphic story encourages readers to imagine what positive anger looks like: it is an active refusal which forces a redrawing of boundaries (the young men flee the scene) but it is not in itself a violence done to others. The ending given to the story, like endings in the stories related in other narratives of the collection, does not engage in imagining permanent solutions or grand narratives of transformation. It is quite simply immersed in the everyday world of momentary negotiations and micro-changes.

Another set of narratives works to show the ways in which discourse is a real space with real effects. In Soumya Menon's 'An Ideal Girl', it is the ever popular world of poster-art typically found on the walls of classrooms, with a narrator reading against the grain of this everyday form by which patriarchy is normalised (characteristics are assigned gender as are vocations and behaviours). In Bhavana Singh's 'I Melanin', it is the advertising associated with the euphemistically labelled 'beauty industry' that is the focus. In Sabhaney's 'Broken Lines', it is the powerful discourses of tradition and modernity by which the contemporary is typically privileged that is the focus. The narrator muses on the synergy between storytelling traditions, which have a practically canonical repertoire to boot, and the December 2012 gang rape. Woman is the absented/invisible of this text, buried beneath layers of reading, and haunts the space generated by the juxtaposition of times – the timeless realm of folk tales versus 2012 – and spaces: the visual storytelling tradition of Bengal (*patachitra*) and 21st-century social and news media.[5] The title page – with black-and-white, vertical, parallel lines broken up by jagged, white, horizontal brush strokes – has the following paragraphs interspersed in the broadest black column on the page, with the last paragraph at the foot of the page, separated from the three others:

> It is difficult for me to keep track of stories these days.
> Having grown up reading books with a clear beginning, middle, and end, stories without a resolution just don't stick.
>
> They tear, and begin to merge hopelessly into one another.
> I first noticed this during the media deluge which followed the gang-rape of a medical student in New Delhi in 2012 ... [ellipsis in original].

Finally, '[But what is] Basic Space?' draws attention to the importance of space, and its interrogation when considering the question of gendered India. It brilliantly displaces the patriarchal architecture of Indian spaces – public/private, political/domestic, familial/individual – by having women, in multiple spaces/realities, ponder the question which gives the graphic story its title: '[But what is] Basic Space?'[6] The title, which is the only verbal element in the first page, shows women's space as a compendium of perspectives on the notion of 'the line' as a 'normal' structuring of identity in patriarchal India.[7] The title and graphic narrative, constituted of multiple stories, open up the core concern of the collection

Thinking gender in 21st-century India 125

with framing gender in contemporary India as a reality configured in demarcated spaces with absolute boundaries that have the force of injunction.

From the ways in which gendered space – a complex of conceptual, physical, psychological, cultural, discursive, emotional and social spheres – structures the stories told in the graphic narratives of *Drawing the Line*, it is possible to conclude the following: a shared concern of the graphic narratives is to make space itself visible, as a structure producing behaviours, actions and gender realities usually hidden in the term 'norm'. I turn my attention now to the ways in which women are imagined handling the worlds in which they find themselves, focusing particularly on stories in which women are active readers and agents of change. In Kanan's 'That's Not Fair', which transforms the womb into the space of a generational shift, the story is of the active refusal and anger of the unborn girl child against the mother, seen doing all she can to ensure her foetus is fair-skinned. This image of desperation is poignant, as the mother is caught between the desire to protect her girl child from social harm (the life that she, as a darker-skinned woman, has faced) and her harming of her unborn child in the process (through her attempts to alter the pigmentation she presumes she has passed on). While the story draws our attention to the unborn child – she is the protagonist and the one who engages in a violent refusal of the gendered world into which she is about to be born – the story is complicated by the mother's story to which it is tethered: the latter is, after all, the familiar image of an Indian woman entirely scripted by the gender violence which makes living with threat (her own and that of daughters she might bear) into a 'normal' reality. In other words, in her life the boundaries by which security (the home) and threat (the outside) are recognised and separated are non-existent.

Priyanka Kumar's 'Ever After', which I have partially discussed above, explores the desires for intimacy (not just sexual) and escape, as a woman engages in fantasies of 'being taken' by a monster.[8] One panel in fact has her intertwined in passion with the monster. This is in stark contrast to the tame domestic life she leads which is brilliantly shown in blurbs: one that depicts a man and a woman speaking, apparently, at cross-purposes – visually inscribed as abstract patterns in lieu of speech from the mouths of the husband and wife at a mealtime with a reverse of the pattern mirrored below the table at which they sit – and another that shows the woman thinking of television and suitcases. Without any comment, the graphic narrative moves through scenes showing the woman sitting in the window (followed, in turn, by a panel in which a two-beaked bird perches on top of a building), having tea with a woman, seeing a monster rise out of the teacup, facing a suitcase bursting with monsters, and finally, a starry landscape with an open, empty suitcase and flag.

My final example, Sabhaney's 'Broken Lines', invites readers to think of the effect of sensational 'news' on individual and collective memory. The graphic narrative juxtaposes the frenzied race to claim authoritative 'representation' of the December 2012 gang rape in the news (in which she is a marginal participant) with the oral-visual storytelling tradition of *patachitra* (the narrative element which provides the segue is her shocking discovery that there is an unsettling continuity between a popular *patachitra* story and the mediatised story of Jyoti Singh). The second half – which juxtaposes visual images in the *patachitra* tradition with authorial interpretation of a tale that is a caution to young *bahus* (daughters-in-law) – is a silent comment on the haunting presence of the past in the present. Interestingly enough, the graphic narrative sets up an intriguing opposition of storytelling genres in the process: if *patachitra*, an art form situated at the crossroads of the visual and the verbal, is a genre traditionally wedded to patriarchal norms, then graphic storytelling, in the hands of 21st-century Indian women, is a genre fully interruptive of it. Furthermore, this narrative clearly invites readers to link contemporary violence against women with Hindu cultural pasts. Finally, the narrative is a powerful confession of the devastating impact of the 2012 gang rape on one individual, a loss of the ability to distinguish fact from fiction and past from present: 'Or have I become so used to stories of unresolved violence that I could see no difference between a mythological tale and a report of a real crime?'

In a collection that identifies the contemporary, and mostly the urban contemporary, as its concern, there is little faith put in transformation – of a permanent sort anyway. Instead, there is a complex patchwork of reality and women's engagement of it. Women slip into a fantasy world, choose escape (the motif of suitcases takes on a particularly powerful and poignant meaning), live complicit lives, or seek ways to disavow the norms to which they are subject. On the one hand we could conclude that 21st-century India in the text shows the dangerous flexibility of a profoundly patriarchal social structure with the capacity to assimilate contemporary technologies, socio-economic transformations and global knowledges into itself (dangerous because it shows a resilience to transformational change). On the other hand, we could recall the exhilaration of Susan's Introduction and its directing of readers to the irreducible variety of women's lived experience, where the latter is imagined as excessive of attempts at containment, whether in discourse or in action.

In the few years since its publication, the collection has attracted some attention, national and international. The first graphic narrative collection of its kind to be published by Zubaan Books, in collaboration with the Goethe Institute at the Delhi branch of Max Muller Bhavan, *Drawing the Line* has been published in North America by Ad Astra Comix (2015), an alternative history comic company founded in Ontario, Canada, by Nicole Marie Burton in 2013. Its website states that its commitment is to 'publish comics with social justice themes' and claims the distinction of publishing the first North American edition of *Drawing the Line* (Ad Astra Comix website, n.d.).

Online reviews show the impact of the collection on the world of readers. One of these reviews historicises the collection by noting the presence of a tradition of globally acknowledged women graphic artists such as Marjane Satrapi, which is furthered by a collection such as *Drawing the Line* ('An Introduction to *Drawing the Line*', n.d.). In the words of the review, the collection has 'showed [*sic*] us that not everyone has to be a professional comic book creator to tell powerful visual stories'. This is a more important observation than it might at first appear to be. Indeed, the original workshop in 2014 appears to have been as much about

Thinking gender in 21st-century India   127

democratising access to the title of graphic artist and the visibility it brings, as it was about de-territorialising the field of gender. Hence it was left entirely up to the workshop participants to settle on an idea and its execution in the full knowledge that the history which impelled the workshop was about as dire as it can get.

On YouTube, a writer using the pen name 'Literally Graphic' posted a five-minute video on *Drawing the Line*, which she describes as 'a collection of very short, very pointed stories about women in India and their experience of gender' and a 'delightful read' ('Drawing the Line Indian Women Fight Back'). In the short video, the reviewer reflects on the personal impact that reading the collection has had. In addition to remarking on the fact that the collection revealed to her the universality of women's experience in sexist societies, she notes that, while the graphic stories offer representative scenes and dramas of gendered experience, figures in the stories do not seem 'generic'. A final comment of hers that I find important concerns the contribution of publishing conditions (alternative, small press) to the reading experience. Indeed, a monograph such as Pavithra Narayanan's *What Are You Reading? The World Market and Indian Literary Production* (2012) impresses on us the very recent nature of the struggle to decolonise reading cultures; this is achieved through the building of an indigenous and multilingual publishing culture reflective of India's internal diversity and without verging on national chauvinism.[9] Zubaan Books is generally acknowledged as an important contributor to this attempt at reshaping the landscape of publishing in India.[10]

In other interesting reviews of *Drawing the Line* that probe the texts in the collection, there are some who have found in the visual landscape of the Indian graphic narrative genre a powerful intervention in the literature that sediments and performs a triumphalist national identity. Emma Dawson Varughese makes a compelling argument for engaging in a hermeneutics that is situated in Indian, rather than Western, ways of seeing and offers a reading of 'The Photo' to establish that it, and others like it across the genre, have developed 'a visuality of the inauspicious', intervening in the visuality of the auspicious[11] that the omnipresent mode of *darshan* keeps in the forefront of the national imaginary.[12] In this countering of the dominant (and preferred) mode of visuality, she argues, the graphic narrative 'disturbs ideas of Indianness in the post-millennial moment' (Dawson Varughese, 2018, 10). What the 'visuality of the inauspicious' captures is histories of gender violence, casteism, communal violence, environmental degradation and the like.

There are other observations that could be made, such as the fact that the narratives in the collection, when approached as a whole, do not hinge social change on the pegs we might expect, such as education, economic improvement and collective action. Policy, that is, along with legislative change, is tangential to the collection's concern with women's daily experience. Legislative and political spheres require other stories and a collection such as this reminds us that political and legislative change, necessary as they are, cannot, and do not, fully contain the issue of a gendered India. Nor is the judicial gaze, which is crudely in evidence behind the sensational calls for chemical castration – that

128 *Sukeshi Kamra*

is, the notion of revenge masked as justice – part of the compass here. The clearing of conceptual space so we can see precisely what it is that the graphic narrative has made its political terrain can be found in Pramod Nayar's *The Indian Graphic Novel: Nation, History and Critique* (2016). He writes: 'Sandra Freitag's argument [is] that civil society's informal activities – as opposed to the state's – especially in the realm of popular visual culture, often challenge the actions of the nation-state' (Nayar, 2016, 191). We could also note that *Drawing the Line* forms part of a project of creating an appetite for 'cultural literacy', as Nayar has argued. He explains that 'critical literacy is central' to processes of countering through 'rupturing the received narratives, histories, and "truths" about India' (Nayar, 2016, 191). I would modify that slightly to say that graphic narratives have as an ambition the *desire* to *produce* an appetite for social and cultural literacy in the middle classes that constitute their readership. This certainly is the hope and ambition of *Drawing the Line*.

In 2018, a second anthology of women's graphic narratives, which featured some of the same participants, was published in English; the German edition appeared a year earlier. Titled *The Elephant in the Room: Women Draw Their World*, the anthology by Spring Collective is described by Manjula Padmanabhan in the Foreword as the second in a series that began with *Drawing the Line* (2018, 5). This time, the workshop in which the graphic stories were generated was held in Nrityagram, an artist enclave in Karnataka, and its participants were from Germany and India. Variety of perspectives, storytelling styles, graphic design, and women graphic storytellers in the 21st century make this anthology as irreducible as *Drawing the Line* to everything but metaphor: line/boundary in the latter and elephants in the room in the former. The collection has the same irreverence for custom, tradition and canons as *Drawing the Line* and it expresses the same desire to show what graphic art and storytelling look like in a far from perfect everyday world. What Padmanabhan says of the collection could easily be argued retrospectively about *Drawing the Line*: here 'the giant, unexamined and unmentionable issues that deform – and sometimes augment – the dreams of so many girls and women' meet 'the unschooled techniques of … amateur cartoonists exploring the digi-verse on their tablets and iPhones' which have, she adds, 'truly revolutionised the visual landscape' (2018, 5).

Notes

1 In India, important categories intersecting with gender are caste, class, familial economy, religion, language and region.
2 In the blurb on her graphic story, titled 'Ever After' for instance, Priyanka Kumar says: 'I like fiction, tea, paint and stories with open endings.'
3 The only pages in *Drawing the Line* that are numbered are those of the Introduction and the Afterword. The Contents page does include the page number on which each graphic narrative begins but since there are no page numbers in the volume itself, I have not mentioned page numbers either.
4 In *Drawing the Line*, Gunjal offers the following comprehensive description of Kali, as a figure of necessary violence: 'Kali is a Hindu goddess associated with Shakti, the

Thinking gender in 21st-century India   129

force of divine female energy. Kali is the fierce avatar of the goddess Durga who, in need of help, summons Kali to combat demons. Kali is the goddess of Time, Change and Destruction, and is often portrayed as dark and violent.'

5 The *patachitra* genre of storytelling in Bengal is one of many forms in which visual and oral text coalesce to relate stories to rural audiences (in *patachitra* the oral is in the form of song). It is an established form of entertainment and stories drawn from the Indian epics, the *Mahabharata* and the *Ramayana*, are part of the repertoire but so are contemporary political conditions.

6 The title is spatially organised as a noun phrase ('Basic Space') with an off-screen, invisible speaker adding the prefix phrase 'But what is'. This play with the notion of a title is important to an understanding of what it is that the graphic story sets out to do: it is both about 'basic' space and an interruptive questioning of it.

7 It is possible that there is an iconic scene from the *Ramayana* that informs the identification of 'the line' as a key metaphor in the story of Indian patriarchy. Sita, Rama's wife, is placed within a protective circle by her husband and his brother Lakshman and instructed to stay within it. Ravana, the figure identified as the villain in the dominant North Indian versions of the *Ramayana*, disguises himself and entices Sita to move out of the circle. As she does so, he abducts her and this act produces the key moral and philosophical moments of the epic.

8 In her bio-note, Kumar says the story is a result of memories of familiar spaces inhabited by the women in the family and a Tamil film dubbed 'Enter the Dragon' after the classic Bruce Lee movie. The act of drawing the story (and the story is only visual with no verbal elements) made her 'dwell upon more things than I'd bargained for – boredom, loneliness, the art of being preoccupied, and the various ways in which we attempt to escape the everyday spaces we inhabit'.

9 See Chapter 3 in particular, 'Fit to Print: The Transnational Publishing Industry' (Narayanan, 2012, 76–112), where Narayanan provides an overview of the publishing houses and commissioning editors of independent India who were trailblazers before moving on to discussing the small independent press industry that dates back to the late 1980s (Narayanan, 2012, 93).

10 In a comprehensive study of the role played by media (mainstream, marginal, commercial, non-commercial, spanning different genres) in the formation and contestation of Indian citizen identity, Lion König discusses the history of alternative mass media genres in independent India, studying self-identified alternative workshops producing alternative graphic stories; a particularly good example is of the *Alag Chitra Katha*, whose history he details, which defines itself in opposition to the powerful comic series, *Amar Chitra Katha* (König, 2016). Dawson Varughese mentions Zubaan Books in her account of the emergence of graphic narratives in 21st-century India with social justice as an objective (Dawson Varughese, 2018, 8).

11 'Visuality' is employed here to speak of the centrality of visual meaning-making to the production of India's contestatory cultural landscape. The phrase of which it is a part, 'visuality of the auspicious', is central to Dawson Varughese's contention that the form of worship across Hinduism's many variants harnesses visuality. In doing so, it produces a very specific form of visual experience, which spills over into cinema, for instance, encouraging Indians to form a similar relationship with screen personalities and actors as it does with deities. The Hindi term that signifies this complex form of visuality is *darshan*.

12 The term *darshan* is not easily rendered into the English language. For an overview of scholarly opinions on the meaning of the term, see Dawson Varughese (2018, 15–16). The clearest definition she provides is of *darshan* as 'essentially the act of seeing wherein the meeting of the eyes connects the gazer and the gazed upon in a multisensory moment of dialogue, both powerful and auspicious' (Dawson Varughese, 2018, 15). It is most typically a term used to describe the relationship with the divine.

Works cited

Ad Astra Comix website (n.d.). 'About Ad Astra Comix: The Panel is Political'. https://adastracomix.com. Accessed 19 November 2018.

Dawson Varughese, Emma (2018). *Visuality and Identity in Post-Millennial Indian Graphic Narratives*. Cham: Palgrave Macmillan.

Guha, Ramachandra (2017). 'India at 70. A Historian's Report Card'. *DC Books*. 17 February. www.youtube.com/watch?v=1WzmdKHQvPE. Accessed 17 December 2018.

'Introduction to Drawing the Line: Indian Women Fight Back' (n.d.). www.stripteasethemag.com/drawing-the-line. Accessed 19 November 2018.

König, Lion (2016). *Cultural Citizenship in India: Politics, Power, and Media*. New Delhi: Oxford University Press.

Kurian, Priya, Larissa Bertonasco, and Ludmilla Bartscht (eds.) (2015). *Drawing the Line: Indian Women Fight Back*. New Delhi: Zubaan Books.

Literally Graphic (2016). 'Drawing the Line Indian Women Fight Back || Anthology Review #Nonfiction #WomenInComics'. *YouTube*. 26 June. www.youtube.com/watch?v=2tY8EzVaN7Q. Accessed 19 November 2018.

Narayanan, Pavithra (2012). *What Are You Reading? The World Market and Indian Literary Production*. New Delhi: Routledge.

Nayar, Pramod K. (2016). *The Indian Graphic Novel: Nation, History and Critique*. London: Routledge.

Padmanabhan, Manjula (2018). 'Foreword'. In: Spring Collective, *The Elephant in the Room: Women Draw Their World*. Delhi: Zubaan Books, p. 5.

Spring Collective (2018). *The Elephant in the Room: Women Draw Their World*. Delhi: Zubaan Books.

Susan, Nisha (2015). 'Introduction'. In: Kurian, Priya, Larissa Bertonasco, and Ludmilla Bartscht (eds.) *Drawing the Line: Indian Women Fight Back*. New Delhi: Zubaan Books, pp. 1–3.

Index

Note: Page numbers in italics indicate figures.

Abbas, Chaudhry Ghulam 36
Abbas, Khwaja Ahmed 18; *Dharti ke Laal (Children of the Earth)* (film) 80
Abdullah, Omar 40
Abdullah, Sheikh 15; and B.P.L. Bedi 29, 30; dismissal of 16, 18–19; as emergency administrator 23; and 'land to the tiller' policy 24–25, 29; methods of 27; and National Conference 27, 36; and 'New Kashmir' project 16, 20; political legacy of 30; *see also* National Conference
Achakzai, Abdul Samad Khan 26–27
Ad Astra Comix 126
Adiga, Aravind: *The White Tiger* 4
Adivasi figure (indigenous person of South Asia) 96
Afghanistan, Islamic militant groups from 37
Agamben, Giorgio 41
Ahmad, Uma Sondhi *112*, 113
Ahmed, Enver: Azad depictions 69; characteristics of work by 73–74; 'Congress Retrievers' 64–65, *65*; early career of 62; 'Indelible Writing on the Wall' 63, *63*; 'Loaves and Fishes' 64, *65*; 'Not yet Master, we still need each other' (cartoon) 63–64, *64*
Alexander, A.V. 62
Alier, Joan Martinez 9, 95
All India Kisan Sabha 24
All-India Progressive Writers' Association 83
'alternative cinema' or 'parallel cinema' 85, 89
Ambai (writer) 92
Ambedkar, B.R. 27, 54

Anand, Mulk Raj 18
Anderson, Perry 50
Andhra Pradesh: Praja Natya Mandali (PNM) in 81, 87–88
animal imagery (in political cartoons) 63, *64–65*, 66, 68–69, 74
Apoorvanand 52
Armed Forces (Special Powers) Act (AFSPA) 38, 43
Association of Parents of Disappeared Persons (APDP) 40; 'Half Widow, Half Wife?' 39
Association of the Parents of Disappeared Persons (APDP) 33
Atali village 52
Attlee, Clement 63
avant-garde film makers 85
Awasthi, Suresh 84
Ayodhya village 49
azaadi (freedom) movement 37
Azad, Abul Kalam 62–66, *63–65*, 69, *71*, 72

Babri Mosque (at Ayodhya) 88
Badaga tribe (in Nilgiris region of Tamil Nadu) 9, 92–93, 97–100
bagh (textile) 113–114, *114*
Bakhtin, Mikhail 49
Balmiki, Ram Avtar 56
Bardhan, Shanti: *Bhookha Hai Bangal (Voice of Bengal)* (play) 80
Bartscht, Ludmilla 117
Batra, Ritesh: *The Lunchbox* (film) 4
Bedi, Baba Pyare Lal (B.P.L.): childhood and education of 17; and CPI 20, 29; detainment of 18; in India 17–18; Korbel on 28–29; at National

Conference session (1945) 27; Nehru on 15; and *New Kashmir* manifesto 7, 16, 19–21, 28; and women's rights in *New Kashmir* manifesto 25
Bedi, Freda 7, 15, 17, 27, 30
Behera, N.C. 37
Benegal, Shayam 85
Bengal: famine in 79–82; storytelling tradition of 124–126, 129n5; violence (1940s) in 67; West 89, 89n2
Bertonasco, Larissa 117
Bhagavad Gita 5
Bharatiya Janata Party (BJP) (or Indian People's Party) 3, 50, 56, 57
Bhardwaj, Dev Prakash 56
Bharucha, Rustom 84
Bhattacharya, Bijon: *Nabanna* (*The New Harvest*) (play) 80–82
Bhutiani, Shubhashish: *Hotel Salvation* (*Mukti Bhawan*) (film) 3–5, 10n1
Bhutto, Benazir 37
Bihar, violence (1940s) in 67
'bio-militarised' bodies 44
Booker/Man Booker Prize 4
Bose, Subhas Chandra 18
Britain: and capitalist development of India 93, 100; and Communism, suppression of 17, 18; Ministry of Information 66; and saviour of India trope 68–69
British Labour Party: *Let Us Face the Future* manifesto 31
Bufacchi, Vittorio 43
Bukhari, S. 36
Burton, Nicole Marie 126
Business Standard 34

Cafaro, Philip 102
Calcutta, famine refugees in 81–82
cartoons and cartoonists 7–8, 73–74; see also Ahmed, Enver; Illingworth, Leslie Gilbert; Shankar
castes, rise of mass organisations for 87; see also specific castes
Cederlöf, Gunnel 93, 96, 102
Cernea, Michael 101
Chandra, K.: *Tragedy of Jinnah* 69
Chargesheet (agit-prop production) 86
Chatterjee, Basu 85
Chattisgarhi traditional forms and techniques 85–86
Chaudhuri, Amit: *A New World* 5
Chhandoke, Neera 42–43

China, disputes with 1, 2
Chinese Revolution 83
Clifford, James 92
climate change 96
Cocteau, Jean: *La Belle et La Bête* 5
collective bargaining 88
colonialism 9, 92–96, 100–103, 127
communalism 3, 7–8, 49, 56, 68
Communism 15, 20
Communist Party of India (CPI) (Maoists): and Bengali famine 79–80; and B.P.L. Bedi 15, 29; and cultural organisations 80; formation of 90n4; and Jana Natya Mandali group 88; *Marxbadi* 83; and Nehruvian project 83; and *New Kashmir* manifesto 7; recruitment efforts of 18; second Congress (1948) 82–83; variable influence of 79–80
Communist Party of India (CPI[M]) (Marxists) 83–84, 86–89, 89n2
Communist Party of India (Marxist-Leninist branches) 83–84, 90n4
Congress Socialist Party 18
constitutional monarchy 21–22
Contemporary India (quarterly) 17–18, 21, 24
Convention on the Protection of All Persons from Enforced Disappearance 41
Cripps, Stafford 62, 67
cultural literacy 128

Daily Mail (newspaper) 61, 66–69
Dalit caste 51, 56, 87
dam projects 95, 101
darshan (visuality) 129nn11–12
Dasgupta, Abani: *Bhookha Hai Bangal* (*Voice of Bengal*) (play) 80
Dawn (newspaper) 8, 61–66, *63–65*
Dawson Varughese, Emma 104–106, 108–109, 111–113, 127, 129nn11–12
Desai, Kiran: *The Inheritance of Loss* 4
Desai, Kishwar: *Witness the Night* 4–6
development refugees 97, 103
Devru/Dewarhu village (in Haryana): and *Hindu Rashtra* 8; Muslims and Hindus in 47–53, 55–56; violence in 51–52
dissent processes 36
Dogra dynasty 22, 27
domestic space 121–123
Drawing the Line (graphic collection) 10, 117–128, 128n3; see also individual authors

Index   133

D'Souza, P. 33
Dutt, Rajani Palme 25–27
Dutt, Utpal 84; *Barricade* (play) 86; *Dushopner Nagari* (*City of Nightmares*) (play) 86

East India Company 93, 102
ecological imperialism 94
ecological nationalism, defined 9
ecological refugees 94, 97
ecosystem people 94, 95
Ehrenburg, Ilya 23
elephant imagery 69, 74; *see also* animal imagery
The Elephant in the Room: Women Draw Their World (graphic collection) 10, 128
emergency proclamation 9, 86–88
enforced disappearances *see* half-widows
English-language novels and diasporic authors 4–5
Enloe, Cynthia: *Bananas, Beaches, and Bases: Making Feminist Sense of International Politics* 34
Enter the Dragon (Tamil film) 129n8
environmental movements 95–96
environmental virtues ethics 101–102
ethnography 92
'eve-teasing' 120

famine 67, 68, 79–82
Fanon, Frantz: *The Wretched of the Earth* 93
Farasat, W. 42
Fascism 81
Fauji (*Soldier*) (film) 55
Ferroukhi, Ismaël: *The Great Journey* (*Le Grand Voyage*) (film) 4
film industry 85
folk performative forms 81, 84
Freitag, Sandra 128
Freud, Sigmund 70
Friends of New Kashmir Committee 30
'the Frontier Gandhi' 27
'full stomach environmentalism' *vs.* 'empty belly environmentalism' 95

Gadar (poet) 88
Gadgil, Madhav 94
Gandhi, Indira 26
Gandhi, Mohandas Karamchand 18, 47, 62, 63, *63–64*, 67, 73
Gandhi, Rajiv 49
Ganguly, S. 36

gay relationships 5
gaz (yardstick) 9–10, 105, 113, 115
ghara (metallic vessel) 9–10, 105, 113, 115
Ghatak, Ritwik 85
global ambitions 2–3
Goethe Institute 126
Gollancz publisher: *India Analysed* (volumes) 23
Golwalkar, M.S. 55
Gopalakrishnan, Kaveri: "Basic Space" 119, 121, 124–125, 129nn6–7
Gould, William 50
Goyal, Seth Manmohan 56
Gramotsav (village festival) 53–56
graphic narratives 10, 117–128
Group Theatre movement (or Naba Natya) 85
Grove, Richard 94
Guha, Ramachandra 9, 94, 95; 'India at 70: A Historian's Report Card' (speech) 118
Guha, Ranajit 101
Gujjari, Zuni 26
Gunjal, Samidha: 'Someday' 120–121, 128–129n4

half-widows (in Jammu and Kashmir): defined 7, 33; injustice and lack of accountability facing 42–44; relief payments to 41; and remarriage 33–34; silencing of 43–44; and state violence 34–35; and unknowability problem 38–42
HarperCollins India 104
Haryana: BJP in, election of 50; Jat caste in 51, 56; *see also* Devru/Dewarhu village
Hashmi, Safdar 87, 88, 90n3
Hedgewar, K.B. 54
heteroglossia 49
The Hiatus Project (blog) 108
Hindu nationalism (or *Hindutva*) 1, 3, 49, 50, 53–56; *see also* Devru/Dewarhu village; Rashtriya Swayamsevak Sangh (RSS) organisation
Hindu Rashtra (Hindu polity, north India) 8, 47, 53, 57
Hindustan Times (newspaper) 8, 62, 69–70, 73

Id-gah (prayer wall) incident (Devru/Dewarhu, 2015) 50–51
Illingworth, Leslie Gilbert 66–69, 73–74

134 Index

illocutionary force 49
'incorporative violence' 8
India: agricultural traditions in 93;
  Constituent Assembly 23–24, 27, 28;
  constitution of 27–28, 38; environmental
  destruction in 93–95; expressions of
  nationality and nationhood in 102; the
  idea of 6, 10; identification documents
  in 54; industrial development in 9; and
  Kashmir conflict 36–38; Lok Sabha
  elections 79; national agenda for culture
  in 84; and *New Kashmir* project 22;
  political and historical context of 2–3
India Analysed (volumes) 23
Indian National Conference 36
Indian National Congress 62, 66, 69–73,
  86, 88
Indian National Planning Commission 23
Indian People's Theatre Association
  (IPTA) 80–82, 84–86, 89
indigenous cultural production 8–9,
  101, 127
infanticide 5
inner lives and secrets 5
Instagram 108
intentionality concept 49
International Covenant on Civil and
  Political Rights (ICCPR) 38
International Relations (IR) discipline
  34–35, 44
iPhones and visual landscape 128
Iqbal, Allama 47, 53
Ishida, Tatsuya: *Sinfest* 117
Islamic militant groups 37

Jain, Kavita 47, 51
Jalali, Pran Nath 20
James, Henry: *The Ambassadors* 5
Jammu: Dogra dynasty in 22; enforced
  disappearances in 38; land redistribution
  in 24–25; National Conference party in
  7, 19; Pashtun tribesmen attack (1947)
  35; Pulwama attack (2019) in 2; security
  forces in 43–44; Sheikh Abdullah as
  prime minister of 27; status of 27–28;
  see also half-widows
Jammu and Kashmir Liberation Front
  (JKLF) 37
Jammu and Kashmir (J&K) National
  Conference 36
Jammu and Kashmir State Human Rights
  Commission (SHRC) 38
Jana Natya Manch (Janam) performance
  group 86, 88, 90n3; *Machine* (play) 87

Jana Natya Mandali performance group 88
Jat caste 47, 51, 56
jatra performative form 86
Jhabvala, Ruth Prawer: *Heat and Dust* 4
Jinnah, Mohamed Ali 61, 64, *65*, 67,
  69–73, *70–72*
Joseph, Anjali: *Saraswati Park* 4, 5
Jumma, Hajji 47–52, 57
Junaid, Tajdar 4
Justice Rajinder Sachar Commission 53

Kalash Yatra 49
Kali (Hindu goddess) 120, 121, 123–124,
  128–129n4
Kamra, Sukeshi 74
Kanan, Harini: 'That's Not Fair' 122, 125
Karnad, Girish 84
Kashmir: accession issue in 22, 35; conflict
  in 2, 35–38; electoral malfeasance
  in 36; enforced disappearances in
  38–39, 42; Hindu landlords in 25;
  land redistribution in 7; leftist groups
  meeting in 18; Pakistani tribal forces'
  invasion (1947) of 22–23; political
  infrastructure of 19; security forces in
  43–44; status of 27–28, 31; violence
  and gendered insecurities in 34–35;
  Women's Self Defence Corps 26;
  see also half-widows
Kaul, Mani 85
Kaushik, Ramesh 47
Kazi, Seema 39
Kemnitz, T.M. 61
Kerala, Left movement in 90n2
Khalidi, Omar: 'Hinduising India:
  secularism in practice' 54
Khan, Khan Abdul Ghaffar 27, *65*, 66
Khan, Liaqat Ali 64, *65*, 69–70, *70*
Khan, Nazmuddin 109–110, *110*
Khan, Pehlu 57
Khan, Rakbar 57
Khilnani, Sunil 6
König, Lion 129n10
Korbel, Josef 28–29
Krishnan, Rajam 92–93; *When the Kurinji
  Blooms* (or *Kurinjithen*) 9, 96–103
Krishnaswamy: *Belchi* (play) 87
Kumar, Priyanka: 'Ever After' 122, 125,
  128n2, 129n8
Kurian, Priya 117
kurinji flower 99

Lalit Kala Akademi for the fine arts 84
land, importance of 93–94

land redistribution 16, 24–25
'land to the tiller' slogan 24
Lawrence, Pethick 62
Left theatre and cultural movement 79, 80, 88; *see also specific parties and groups*
liberalisation, privatisation and globalisation (LPG) policies 2, 85, 88, 89
'Literally Graphic' (writer's pseudonym) 127
Little Theatre Group (LTG): *The Special Train* (play) 86
Low, David 73
Ludden, David 101

maang-tikka 115, *115*
Mahabharata (Indian epic) 129n5
Maharaj, Kapil Muni 56
Malhotra, Aanchal *112*; on objects and material memory 104–106; *Remnants of a Separation* 9–10, 104–115, *107*
Maoist Communist Centre 90
marginalised groups 2, 34
marriage photo genre 121–122
martyrdom 55
media coverage of events 10, 129n10
memory *see* objects and material memory
Menon, Soumya: 'An Ideal Girl' 124
might is right ('*jiski lathi, uski bhains*') paradigm 49
Mill, John Stuart: *On Liberty* 43
mimicry techniques 70
misogyny and violence against women 5; *see also* women and gender issues
Mistry, Diti: 'Bombay Local' 120, 121
Mitra, Shombhu 81, 85
modernity: aesthetic responses to 3–6; global North's claim to 118; in Gunjal's 'Someday' 123; in Sabhaney's 'Broken Lines' 124
Modi, Narendra 3, 57; and communal violence 3; independence-day address (2017) 1
Mohammad, Bakshi Ghulam 30
Mohanty, Chandra Talpade 34–35, 44
Mookumalai dam project 101
Mukul, Akshaya 50
Muley/Mola/Mula Jats 47, 52
Mumbai 120
Muslim communities: collective identity of 62; in Devru/Dewarhu 47–53, 55–56; Gujjar 52; marginalisation of 2; as 'political category' 51; and public prayer 8; statistics on 53; Suhrawardy on 68; treatment of 53

Muslim Conference 16, 22
Muslim League 8, 22, 61–64, 66–67, 69–73
Muslim United Front (MUF) 36

Naba Natya (or Group Theatre movement) 85
Nagarjun, Baba 83
Narayanan, Pavithra: *What Are You Reading? The World Market and Indian Literary Production* 127, 129n9
Narayanan, Uma 98
National Conference (Kashmiri nationalist party): annual session (1945) 26; and B.P.L. Bedi 16; and commission on constitutional change (1943) 19; flag of 25–26; motivations of 23; national project for Kashmir 22; and women, appealing to 25–26; *see also* Jammu and Kashmir (J&K) National Conference; *New Kashmir* manifesto
National Democratic Alliance 50
nationalism and parochialism 2–3
National School of Drama (NSD) 84
Nayar, Pramod: *The Indian Graphic Novel: Nation, History and Critique* 128
Naya Theatre 85
negative action and negative causation 43
Nehru, Jawaharlal: on B.P.L. Bedi 15; depictions of *63*, 63–67, *65*; development vision of 95–96; on Kashmir's accession 35–36; at National Conference session (1945) 26; and Sheikh Abdullah 18
'Nehruvian socialism' 83, 86
New Kashmir manifesto: adoption of 26; as developmental roadmap 28; economic and agricultural plan of 24; effects of 30–31; introduction to 23; purpose of 21, 23, 28; and Stalin Constitution 21–22
Nilgiris region (Tamil Nadu) 92; *see also* Badaga tribe
Nixon, Rob 95–97
non-governmental organisations (NGOs) 89
North-West Frontier Province (NWFP) 35

OBC status 51
objects and material memory 9–10, 105–115
Olapally, D.M. 36
omission, violence by 43
overhead shots (cinematic technique) 4

136 *Index*

Padmanabhan, Chitra 74
Padmanabhan, Manjula 128
Pakistan: conflict with 1, 2; Directorate of Inter-Service Intelligence (ISI) 37; establishment of 67; and Kashmir 22; Malhotra in 109
Pakistan Times (newspaper) 8
Pant, Pandit 65
'parallel cinema' or 'alternative cinema' 85, 89
Partition 7, 27, 48, 104–111, 113–115
Pashtun tribesmen 35
patachitra (storytelling tradition) 124–126, 129n5
Patel, Vallabhai 63, 63–66, 65, 68
peasants and the working class 18, 24, 29, 81, 84, 86–87, 93–97
People's Little Theatre 86
people trafficking 5
phulkari fabric 113–114
pigmentation, altering 122, 125
postcolonial feminism 35
power relations 34–35, 92
Praja Natya Mandali (PNM) 81, 87–88
Premchand, Munshi 90n3
print culture, power of 74
Progressive Writers Association (PWA) 81
'public rites' and 'patriotic funerals' performances 57
public space 122–123
Pulwama attack (February 2019) 2
Punjab: peasants' movement in 24; violence (1940s) in 67; Western 35
Purushotham, S. 48
Pykara Dam (in Nilgiris region of Tamil Nadu) 9, 98

Quit India campaign 18, 22, 62, 79
Quit Kashmir campaign 22, 27
Qutab, Soudiya 38–39

racism *vs.* communalism 68
Raina, N.N. 26
Ramayana (Indian epic) 129n5, 129n7
Ram Janmabhoomi Movement 49
Ranadive, B.T. 83
Rashtriya Swayamsevak Sangh (RSS) organisation 3, 50–52, 54–56
Ray, Satyajit 85; *Aparajito* (film) 4
reading cultures, decolonising 127
Residential Mosque ('*Rihayashi Masjid*') (Devru/Dewarhu) 48–49
resource omnivores 94

river valley development 95
Rohtak refugee camp 53
Roy, Arundhati: *The God of Small Things* 4
Rushdie, Salman: *Midnight's Children* 4
Russia Today Society 21
Russo, Ann 34–35

Sabhaney, Vidyun: 'Broken Lines' 119, 124–126
Sadiq, G.M. 29
Safdar Hashmi Memorial Trust (SAHMAT) 88
Sahitya Akademi for literature 84
Sahni, Balraj 18
Said, Edward 69
Saini, Nayab Singh 54, 56
Samudaya (cultural organisation) 87
Sandler, Ronald 102
Sangeet Natak Akademi (SNA) 8–9, 84
Sarabhai, Mridula 30
Saraf, M.Y. 20
Saraswati (Hindu goddess) 5
Sathe, Anna Bhau 81
Satrapi, Marjane 126
Sayeed, Mufti Mohammed 40
Scheduled and Other Backward Castes categories 47
Scott, Paul: *Staying On* 4
Second World War 18–19, 62, 79
secularity 51
security politics and militarisation 42–44
Seetharam, Prema 98
Sehanabis, Chinmohan 83
self-sacrifice (in colonial land acquisition) 97, 101
Sen, Mrinal 85
senses and memory 111
Seth, Deepani: 'The Walk' 119, 122–123
sexism 68; *see also* women and gender issues
Shah, K.T. 23–24
Shah, Waris 113
Shaheed (film) 57
Shahni, Kumar 85
Shakespeare, William: *Romeo and Juliet* (play) 5
Shankar 69–74, *70–72*
Shimla talks 64–65
Singh, Bhavana: 'I Melanin' 124
Singh, Gursharan 87
Singh, Hari 35
Singh, Jyoti 10, 117–119, 124–126

Singh, Maharaja Hari 19
Singh, Reshu: 'The Photo' 121–122
Singh, Sobha 26
Sivaramakrishnan, K. 93, 96, 102
Skinner, Quentin 49
S.K. Patel Film Enquiry Committee 85
slow violence 95, 96
social media and internet as borderless 108–109
Sombart, Werner 17
Soviet Union: and pro-Soviet theme of *New Kashmir* manifesto 23; Stalin Constitution 16, 20–21, 25
Spring Collective 128
street theatre 83, 86–89
Subaltern Studies movement 101
Suhrawardy 68, 69
Susan, Nisha 117, 126

tamasha performances 81
Tanvir, Habib 84–86, 90n3
Taylor, Imogen 109
Taylor, John Grigor 109
Tebhaga movement 83
Telengana rebellions 29, 83, 88
Tendulkar, Vijay 84
terrorist organisations 37
Thapar, Romesh 57
Tharoor, Shashi 104
Tharra village 52
Theatre Union (women's group) 87
Torres, Lourdes 34–35
Tribune (newspaper) 8
Tripura, Left movement in 89–90n2
Truffaut, François: *The 400 Blows* 5

UNHCR: 'The State of the World's Refugees' report (2009) 105
United Provinces, violence (1940s) in 67

Unny, E.P. 74
Upanishads 5
urban elites 94
Uttar Pradesh (UP): displaced people from 47; language used in 50

Vachani, Lalit: *The Boy in the Branch* (film) 55
Vajpayee, Atal Bihari 54
Varanasi (city) 3–4
Verma, Rahul: *Zahreeli Hawa* (play) 86, 90n3
Village Republic (of RSS) 54–57
Vishwa Hindu Parishad 49
visuality 127, 129n11

wealth inequality 2
Western radical and liberal feminist scholarship 34–35
Wickham 68
Wilcox, Lauren 41
Wilder, Billy: *The Apartment* (film) 4
Winchell, S.P. 37
witnessing, act of 118
women and gender issues: in graphic narratives 117–128; in and intersecting categories 128n1; *New Kashmir* manifesto 25–26, 28; in political cartoons 68, 72; and power relations 34–35; rise of mass organisations for 87; and security concerns 121–122; and sexual violence and harassment 117–120, 124–126; and state violence 34; in Western radical and liberal feminist scholarship 34–35; in *Witness the Night* 5–6; *see also* 'half-widows'

Zubaan Books 126, 129n10

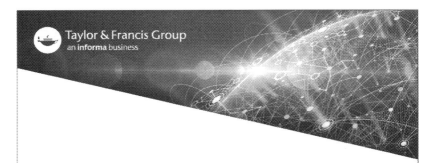

Printed in the United States
By Bookmasters